Insights You Need from
Harvard
Business
Review

ARTIFICIAL
INTELLIGENCE

Insights You Need from Harvard Business Review

Business is changing. Will you adapt or be left behind?

Get up to speed and deepen your understanding of the topics that are shaping your company's future with the **Insights You Need from Harvard Business Review** series. Featuring HBR's smartest thinking on fast-moving issues—blockchain, cybersecurity, AI, and more—each book provides the foundational introduction and practical case studies your organization needs to compete today and collects the best research, interviews, and analysis to get it ready for tomorrow.

You can't afford to ignore how these issues will transform the landscape of business and society. The Insights You Need series will help you grasp these critical ideas—and prepare you and your company for the future.

Books in the series include:

Agile

Artificial Intelligence

Blockchain

Cybersecurity

Monopolies and Tech Giants

Strategic Analytics

Insights You Need from
Harvard Business Review

ARTIFICIAL INTELLIGENCE

Harvard Business Review Press
Boston, Massachusetts

HBR Press Quantity Sales Discounts

Harvard Business Review Press titles are available at significant quantity discounts when purchased in bulk for client gifts, sales promotions, and premiums. Special editions, including books with corporate logos, customized covers, and letters from the company or CEO printed in the front matter, as well as excerpts of existing books, can also be created in large quantities for special needs.

For details and discount information for both print and ebook formats, contact booksales@harvardbusiness.org, tel. 800-988-0886, or www.hbr.org/bulksales.

The web addresses referenced in this book were live and correct at the time of the book's publication but may be subject to change.

Library of Congress Cataloging-in-Publication Data

Title: Artificial intelligence : the insights you need from Harvard Business Review.
Other titles: Artificial intelligence (Harvard Business Review Press) | Insights you need from Harvard Business Review.
Description: Boston, Massachusetts : Harvard Business Review Press, [2019] | Series: The insights you need from Harvard Business Review
Identifiers: LCCN 2019011886 | ISBN 978-1-63369-827-7
Subjects: LCSH: Artificial intelligence. | Artificial intelligence—Industrial applications. | Technological innovations—Economic aspects.
Classification: LCC Q335 .A778 2019 | DDC 658/.0563—dc23
LC record available at https://lccn.loc.gov/2019011886

Contents

Contents

Contents

Introduction

THE STATE OF AI IN BUSINESS

by Thomas H. Davenport

The most important general-purpose technology of our era is artificial intelligence. So Eric Brynjolfsson and Andrew McAfee describe AI in the first article of this book. But even as the significance of AI becomes irrefutable, it remains misunderstood. Executives view AI as a key disruptive technology, employees fear it as a job destroyer, consultants pitch it as a cure-all, and the media hype and deride it endlessly.

This book will help you tune out all this noise and understand AI's implications for you and your business. No matter your industry, level, or the size of your company, this collection of some of HBR's best recent articles on AI will show you where the technology is going.

Let's start with an overview of the state of AI in business today and its near-term implications.

AI *is* undoubtedly booming in business—at least in certain segments of it. In my work, I've helped design and analyze surveys suggesting that 25% to 30% of large U.S. companies are pursuing AI, many quite aggressively. Some have hundreds or even thousands of projects underway. The firms using AI most aggressively are large businesses with the most data—online platforms, financial services, telecommunications, and retail. Small- to medium-sized enterprises, business-to-business firms, and those in basic manufacturing industries are less likely to use AI. They typically lack not only the data to succeed with AI, but the expertise and awareness to pursue it effectively. Firms outside the United States are also pursuing AI at a slower pace, although there are aggressive adopters in China, the U.K., Canada, and Singapore.

A variety of different AI technologies are in use. You need to be aware of which ones do what. As Emma Martinho-Truswell explains in her article, machine learning is perhaps the most important component of AI, but it has multiple variations—ordinary statistical machine learning, neural networks, deep learning neural networks, and so on. Versions of AI also use semantic approaches to understanding language and logic-based rule engines for making simple decisions. Each technology performs a particular set of tasks; deep learning, for example, excels at recognizing images and speech.

AI is being applied for various business purposes. The most common uses enable us to make better decisions, improve operational processes, and enhance products and services. The first two are an extension of business analytics and typically employ machine learning; product-oriented objectives are common in high-tech firms, automobiles, and advanced manufacturing.

Many large companies are creating infrastructures and processes to manage AI. More than a third of large U.S. firms report in multiple surveys that they have a strategy in place for AI, have created a center of excellence to facilitate its use, and have identified its champions in the management team. As Vikram Mahidhar and I suggest in our article, late adopters may have difficulty catching up.

Companies are finding success by focusing their AI efforts in certain areas of the organization. Given the combination of short-term incremental value and long-term opportunity, many companies are tempering expectations about AI while still providing motivation to move forward aggressively with the technology. This is perhaps best accomplished by undertaking several projects focused in a particular area rather than spreading AI projects throughout the organization. Transforming customer service, for example, might include projects involving chatbots, intelligent agents, recommendation engines, and so forth.

AI hasn't transformed business—yet. While surveys suggest high expectations for transformation and high percentages of respondents say they have achieved economic returns, there are few examples of sweeping business reinvention thus far, for several reasons:

- It's still early in the life cycle of AI activity.

- Not every company has data that's suited for AI, as Ajay Agrawal, Joshua Gans, and Avi Goldfarb explain in their article (although H. James Wilson, Paul Daugherty, and my son Chase Davenport suggest in their article that data requirements for effective AI may lessen in the future).

- Companies are undertaking pilots with AI rather than production deployments, as Andrew Ng recommends in his piece.

- AI tends to be a narrow technology that supports particular tasks, not entire jobs or processes.

- Highly ambitious moon-shot projects, such as treating cancer, enabling autonomous vehicles, and powering drone deliveries, have been unsuccessful or slow to arrive.

Even at data powerhouses like Amazon, most AI activity has involved projects that "quietly but meaningfully improve core operations," according to CEO Jeff Bezos in his 2017 letter to shareholders. It's an evolutionary set of improvements that will eventually add up to revolution.

AI's overall impact on employment isn't certain, but jobs will clearly change. Some observers have predicted dire levels of AI-driven unemployment. Thus far—as Wilson and Daugherty discuss in their article on "collaborative intelligence"—augmentation of human work by smart machines has been far more common than large-scale automation. Therefore, according to Mark Knickrehm, organizations need to begin preparing employees to work alongside smart machines and add value to their efforts.

Implementing AI raises ethical questions. Other articles in the book, including one by Roman Yampolskiy, suggest that it's not too early to consider the ethical concerns around AI. Algorithmic bias and lack of transparency are two critical issues that AI exacerbates. These powerful technologies have powerful implications for the workplace and the broader society.

With these fundamentals covered, it's time to dive into the articles. To best understand how AI will impact your company's situation, consider these questions as you read:

- Which particular AI technologies have the greatest potential benefit to your organization?

- How might those technologies enable new strategies, business models, or business process designs?

- What data resources do you have—or might you obtain—in order to power AI projects?

- How do you anticipate that AI will impact your workforce, and how can you begin to prepare employees to augment AI capabilities?

If you and your organization haven't already confronted these questions, let this book spark conversations. Think about how the right AI initiative could help your division perform better or make you more efficient at your own job. Simply asking the questions may be the first step in starting your company down the path of transformation.

As a professor and a consultant on information technology and business, I've spent the past several decades watching AI alternate from spring blooms to winter doldrums. This time is different. AI is deeply ensconced in business and is starting to bring about exciting change. Now, it appears that winter will not return.

Section 1

UNDERSTANDING AI AND MACHINE LEARNING

1

THE BUSINESS OF ARTIFICIAL INTELLIGENCE

by Erik Brynjolfsson and Andrew McAfee

For more than 250 years the fundamental drivers of economic growth have been technological innovations. The most important of these are what economists call general-purpose technologies—a category that includes the steam engine, electricity, and the internal combustion engine. Each one catalyzed waves of complementary innovations and opportunities. The internal combustion engine, for example, gave rise to cars, trucks, airplanes, chain saws, and lawnmowers, along with big-box retailers, shopping centers, cross-docking warehouses, new supply chains, and, when you think about it, suburbs. Companies as diverse as Walmart, UPS, and Uber found ways to leverage the technology to create profitable new business models.

The most important general-purpose technology of our era is artificial intelligence, particularly machine learning (ML)—that is, the machine's ability to keep improving its performance without humans having to explain exactly how to accomplish all the tasks it's given. Within just the past few years machine learning has become far more effective and widely available. We can now build systems that learn how to perform tasks on their own.

Why is this such a big deal? Two reasons. First, we humans know more than we can tell: We can't explain exactly how we're able to do a lot of things—from recognizing a face to making a smart move in the ancient Asian strategy game of Go. Prior to ML, this inability to articulate our own knowledge meant that we couldn't automate many tasks. Now we can.

Second, ML systems are often excellent learners. They can achieve superhuman performance in a wide range of activities, including detecting fraud and diagnosing disease. Excellent digital learners are being deployed across the economy, and their impact will be profound.

In the sphere of business, AI is poised to have a transformational impact, on the scale of earlier general-purpose technologies. Although it is already in use in thousands of companies around the world, most big opportunities have not yet been tapped. The effects of AI will be magnified in the coming decade, as manufacturing, retailing, transportation, finance, health care, law, advertising, insurance, entertainment, education, and virtually every other industry transform their core processes and business models to take advantage of machine learning. The bottleneck now is in management, implementation, and business imagination.

Like so many other new technologies, however, AI has generated lots of unrealistic expectations. We see business plans liberally sprinkled with references to machine learning, neural nets, and other forms of the technology, with little connection to its real capabilities. Simply calling a dating site "AI-powered," for example, doesn't make it any more effective, but it might help with fund-raising. This article will cut through the noise to describe the real potential of AI, its practical implications, and the barriers to its adoption.

What Can AI Do Today?

The term *artificial intelligence* was coined in 1955 by John McCarthy, a math professor at Dartmouth who organized the seminal conference on the topic the following year. Ever since, perhaps in part because of its evocative name, the field has given rise to more than its share of fantastic claims and promises. In 1957 the economist Herbert Simon predicted that computers would beat humans at chess within 10 years. (It took 40.) In 1967 the cognitive scientist Marvin Minsky said, "Within a generation the problem of creating 'artificial intelligence' will be substantially solved." Simon and Minsky were both intellectual giants, but they erred badly. Thus it's understandable that dramatic claims about future breakthroughs meet with a certain amount of skepticism.

Let's start by exploring what AI is already doing and how quickly it is improving. The biggest advances have been in two broad areas: perception and cognition. In the former category some of the most practical advances have been made in relation to speech. Voice recognition is still far from perfect, but millions of people are now using it—think Siri, Alexa, and Google Assistant. The text you are now reading was originally dictated to a computer and transcribed with sufficient accuracy to make it faster than typing. A study by the Stanford computer scientist James Landay and colleagues found that speech recognition is now about three times as fast, on average, as typing on a cell phone. The error rate, once 8.5%, has dropped to 4.9%. What's striking is that this substantial improvement has come not over the past 10 years but just since the summer of 2016.

Image recognition, too, has improved dramatically. You may have noticed that Facebook and other apps now recognize many of your friends' faces in posted photos and prompt you to tag them with their names. An app running on your smartphone will recognize virtually any bird in the wild. Image recognition is even replacing ID cards at corporate headquarters. Vision systems, such as those used in self-driving cars, formerly made a mistake when identifying a pedestrian as often as once in 30 frames (the cameras in these systems record about 30 frames a second); now they err less often than once in 30 million frames. The error rate for recognizing images from a large database called ImageNet, with several million photographs of common, obscure, or downright weird images, fell from higher than 30% in 2010 to about 4% in 2016 for the best systems. (See figure 1-1.)

The speed of improvement has accelerated rapidly in recent years as a new approach, based on very large or "deep" neural nets, was adopted. The ML approach for

FIGURE 1-1

Machines have made real strides in distinguishing among similar-looking categories of images

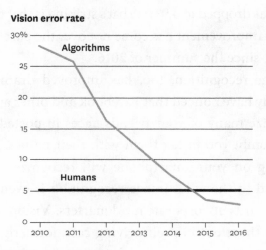

Vision error rate

Source: Electronic Frontier Foundation

vision systems is still far from flawless—but even people have trouble quickly recognizing puppies' faces or, more embarrassingly, see their cute faces where none exist.

The second type of major improvement has been in cognition and problem solving. Machines have already beaten the finest (human) players of poker and Go—achievements that experts had predicted would take at least another decade. Google's DeepMind team has used ML systems to improve the cooling efficiency at data centers by more than 15%, even after they were optimized by human experts. Intelligent agents are being used by the cybersecurity company Deep Instinct to detect malware, and by PayPal to prevent money laundering. A system using IBM technology automates the claims process at an insurance company in Singapore, and a system from Lumidatum, a data science platform firm, offers timely advice to improve customer support. Dozens of companies are using ML to decide which trades to execute on Wall Street, and more and more credit decisions are made with its help. Amazon employs ML to optimize inventory and improve product recommendations to customers. Infinite Analytics developed one ML system to predict whether a user would click on a particular ad, improving online ad placement for a global consumer packaged goods company, and another to improve customers' search and discovery process at a Brazilian online retailer. The first system increased advertising ROI threefold, and the second resulted in a $125 million increase in annual revenue.

Machine learning systems are not only replacing older algorithms in many applications, but are now superior at many tasks that were once done best by humans. Although the systems are far from perfect, their error rate—about 5%—on the ImageNet database is at or better than human-level performance. Voice recognition, too, even in noisy environments, is now nearly equal to human performance. Reaching this threshold opens up vast new possibilities for transforming the workplace and the economy. Once AI-based systems surpass human performance at a given task, they are much likelier to spread quickly. For instance, Aptonomy and Sanbot, makers respectively of drones and robots, are using improved vision systems to automate much of the work of security guards. The software company Affectiva, among others, is using them to recognize emotions such as joy, surprise, and anger in focus groups. And Enlitic is one of several deep-learning startups that use them to scan medical images to help diagnose cancer.

These are impressive achievements, but the applicability of AI-based systems is still quite narrow. For instance, their remarkable performance on the ImageNet database, even with its millions of images, doesn't always translate into similar success "in the wild," where lighting conditions, angles, image resolution, and context may be very different. More fundamentally, we can marvel at a system that understands Chinese speech and translates it into English, but we don't expect such a system to know what a particular Chinese character means—let alone where to eat in Beijing. If someone performs a task well, it's natural to assume that the person has some competence in related tasks. But ML systems are trained to do specific tasks, and typically their knowledge does not generalize. The fallacy that a computer's narrow understanding implies broader understanding is perhaps the biggest source of confusion, and exaggerated claims, about AI's progress. We are far from machines that exhibit general intelligence across diverse domains.

Understanding Machine Learning

The most important thing to understand about ML is that it represents a fundamentally different approach to creating software: The machine learns from examples, rather than being explicitly programmed for a particular outcome. This is an important break from previous practice. For most of the past 50 years, advances in information technology and its applications have focused on codifying existing knowledge and procedures and embedding them in machines. Indeed, the term "coding" denotes the painstaking process of transferring knowledge from developers' heads into a form that machines can understand and execute. This approach has a fundamental weakness: Much of the knowledge we all have is tacit, meaning that we can't fully explain it. It's nearly impossible for us to write down instructions that would enable another person to learn how to ride a bike or to recognize a friend's face.

In other words, we all know more than we can tell. This fact is so important that it has a name: Polanyi's Paradox, for the philosopher and polymath Michael Polanyi, who described it in 1964. Polanyi's Paradox not only limits what we can tell one another but has historically placed a fundamental restriction on our ability to endow machines with intelligence. For a long time that limited the activities that machines could productively perform in the economy.

Machine learning is overcoming those limits. In this second wave of the second machine age, machines built by humans are learning from examples and using structured feedback to solve on their own problems such as Polanyi's classic one of recognizing a face.

Different Flavors of Machine Learning

Artificial intelligence and machine learning come in many flavors, but most of the successes in recent years have been in one category: supervised learning systems, in which the machine is given lots of examples of the correct answer to a particular problem. This process almost always involves mapping from a set of inputs, X, to a set of outputs, Y. For instance, the inputs might be pictures of various animals, and the correct outputs might be labels for those animals: dog, cat, horse. The inputs could also be waveforms from a sound recording and the outputs could be words: "yes," "no," "hello," "good-bye." (See table 1-1.)

Successful systems often use a training set of data with thousands or even millions of examples, each of which has been labeled with the correct answer. The system can then be let loose to look at new examples. If the training has gone well, the system will predict answers with a high rate of accuracy.

The algorithms that have driven much of this success depend on an approach called *deep learning*, which uses

TABLE 1-1

Supervised learning systems

As two pioneers in the field, Tom Mitchell and Michael I. Jordan, have noted, most of the recent progress in machine learning involves mapping from a set of inputs to a set of outputs. Some examples:

Input X	Output Y	Application
Voice recording	Transcript	Speech recognition
Historical market data	Future market data	Trading bots
Photograph	Caption	Image tagging
Drug chemical properties	Treatment efficacy	Pharma R&D
Store transaction details	Is the transaction fraudulent?	Fraud detection
Recipe ingredients	Customer reviews	Food recommendations
Purchase histories	Future purchase behavior	Customer retention
Car locations and speed	Traffic flow	Traffic lights
Faces	Names	Face recognition

neural networks. Deep learning algorithms have a significant advantage over earlier generations of ML algorithms: They can make better use of much larger data sets. The old systems would improve as the number of examples in the training data grew, but only up to a point, after which additional data didn't lead to better predictions. According to Andrew Ng, one of the giants of the field, deep neural nets don't seem to level off in this way: More data leads to better and better predictions. Some very large systems are trained by using 36 million examples or more. Of course, working with extremely large data sets requires more and more processing power, which is one reason the very big systems are often run on supercomputers or specialized computer architectures.

Any situation in which you have a lot of data on behavior and are trying to predict an outcome is a potential application for supervised learning systems. Jeff Wilke, who leads Amazon's consumer business, says that supervised learning systems have largely replaced the memory-based filtering algorithms that were used to make personalized recommendations to customers. In other cases, classic algorithms for setting inventory levels and optimizing supply chains have been replaced by more efficient and robust systems based on machine learning. JPMorgan Chase introduced a system for reviewing commercial loan contracts; work that used to take loan officers 360,000 hours can now be done in a few seconds. And supervised learning systems are now being used to diagnose skin cancer. These are just a few examples.

It's comparatively straightforward to label a body of data and use it to train a supervised learner; that's why supervised ML systems are more common than *unsu*pervised ones, at least for now. Unsupervised learning systems seek to learn on their own. We humans are excellent unsupervised learners: We pick up most of our knowledge of the world (such as how to recognize a tree) with little or no labeled data. But it is exceedingly difficult to develop a successful machine learning system that works this way.

If and when we learn to build robust unsupervised learners, exciting possibilities will open up. These machines could look at complex problems in fresh ways to help us discover patterns—in the spread of diseases, in price moves across securities in a market, in customers' purchase behaviors, and so on—that we are currently unaware of. Such possibilities lead Yann LeCun, the head of AI research at Facebook and a professor at NYU, to compare supervised learning systems to the frosting on the cake and unsupervised learning to the cake itself.

Another small but growing area within the field is *reinforcement learning*. This approach is embedded in systems that have mastered Atari video games and board games like Go. It is also helping to optimize data center power usage and to develop trading strategies for the stock market. Robots created by Kindred use machine learning to identify and sort objects they've never encountered before, speeding up the "pick and place" process in distribution centers for consumer goods. In reinforcement learning systems the programmer specifies the current state of the system and the goal, lists allowable actions, and describes the elements of the environment that constrain the outcomes for each of those actions. Using the allowable actions, the system has to figure out how to get as close to the goal as possible. These systems work well when humans can specify the goal but not necessarily how to get there. For instance, Microsoft used reinforcement learning to select headlines for MSN.com news stories by "rewarding" the system with a higher score when more visitors clicked on the link. The system tried to maximize its score on the basis of the rules its designers gave it. Of course, this means that a reinforcement learning system will optimize for the goal you explicitly reward, not necessarily the goal you really care about (such as lifetime customer value), so specifying the goal correctly and clearly is critical.

Putting Machine Learning to Work

There are three pieces of good news for organizations looking to put ML to use today. First, AI skills are spreading quickly. The world still has not nearly enough data scientists and machine learning experts, but the demand for them is being met by online educational resources as well as by universities. The best of these, including Udacity, Coursera, and fast.ai, do much more than teach introductory concepts; they can actually get smart, motivated students to the point of being able to create industrial-grade ML deployments. In addition to training their own people, interested companies can use online talent platforms such as Upwork, Topcoder, and Kaggle to find ML experts with verifiable expertise.

The second welcome development is that the necessary algorithms and hardware for modern AI can be bought or rented as needed. Google, Amazon, Microsoft, Salesforce, and other companies are making powerful ML infrastructure available via the cloud. The cutthroat competition among these rivals means that companies that want to experiment with or deploy ML will see more and more capabilities available at ever-lower prices over time.

The final piece of good news, and probably the most underappreciated, is that you may not need all that much data to start making productive use of ML. The performance of most machine learning systems improves as they're given more data to work with, so it seems logical to conclude that the company with the most data will win. That might be the case if "win" means "dominate the global market for a single application such as ad targeting or speech recognition." But if success is defined instead as significantly improving performance, then sufficient data is often surprisingly easy to obtain.

For example, Udacity cofounder Sebastian Thrun noticed that some of his salespeople were much more effective than others when replying to inbound queries in a chat room. Thrun and his graduate student Zayd Enam realized that their chat room logs were essentially a set of labeled training data—exactly what a supervised learning system needs. Interactions that led to a sale were labeled successes, and all others were labeled failures. Zayd used the data to predict what answers successful salespeople were likely to give in response to certain very common inquiries and then shared those predictions with the other salespeople to nudge them toward better performance. After 1,000 training cycles, the salespeople had increased their effectiveness by 54% and were able to serve twice as many customers at a time.

The AI startup WorkFusion takes a similar approach. It works with companies to bring higher levels of automation to back-office processes such as paying international invoices and settling large trades between financial institutions. The reason these processes haven't been automated yet is that they're complicated; relevant information isn't always presented the same way every time ("How do we know what currency they're talking about?"), and some interpretation and judgment are necessary. WorkFusion's software watches in the background as people do their work and uses their actions as training data for the cognitive task of classification ("This invoice is in dollars. This one is in yen. This one is in euros . . ."). Once the system is confident enough in its classifications, it takes over the process.

Machine learning is driving changes at three levels: tasks and occupations, business processes, and business models. An example of task-and-occupation redesign is the use of machine vision systems to identify potential cancer cells—freeing up radiologists to focus on truly critical cases, to communicate with patients, and to coordinate with other physicians. An example of process redesign is the reinvention of the workflow and layout of Amazon fulfillment centers after the introduction of robots and optimization algorithms based on machine learning. Similarly, business models need to be rethought to take advantage of ML systems that can intelligently recommend music or movies in a personalized way. Instead of selling songs à la carte on the basis of consumer choices, a better model might offer a subscription to a personalized station that predicted and played music a particular customer would like, even if the person had never heard it before.

Note that machine learning systems hardly ever replace the entire job, process, or business model. Most often they complement human activities, which can make their work ever more valuable. The most effective rule for the new division of labor is rarely, if ever, "give all tasks to the machine." Instead, if the successful completion of a process requires 10 steps, one or two of them may become automated while the rest become more valuable for humans to do. For instance, the chat room sales support system at Udacity didn't try to build a bot that could take over all the conversations; rather, it advised human salespeople about how to improve their performance. The humans remained in charge but became vastly more effective and efficient. This approach is usually much more feasible than trying to design machines that can do everything humans can do. It often leads to better, more satisfying work for the people involved and ultimately to a better outcome for customers.

Designing and implementing new combinations of technologies, human skills, and capital assets to meet customers' needs requires large-scale creativity and planning. It is a task that machines are not very good at. That makes being an entrepreneur or a business manager one of society's most rewarding jobs in the age of ML.

Risks and Limits

The second wave of the second machine age brings with it new risks. In particular, machine learning systems often have low "interpretability," meaning that humans have difficulty figuring out how the systems reached their decisions. Deep neural networks may have hundreds of millions of connections, each of which contributes a small amount to the ultimate decision. As a result, these systems' predictions tend to resist simple, clear explanation. Unlike humans, machines are not (yet!) good storytellers. They can't always give a rationale for why a particular applicant was accepted or rejected for a job, or a particular medicine was recommended. Ironically, even as we have begun to overcome Polanyi's Paradox, we're facing a kind of reverse version: Machines know more than they can tell us.

This creates three risks. First, the machines may have hidden biases, derived not from any intent of the designer but from the data provided to train the system. For instance, if a system learns which job applicants to accept for an interview by using a data set of decisions made by human recruiters in the past, it may inadvertently learn to perpetuate their racial, gender, ethnic, or other biases. Moreover, these biases may not appear as an explicit rule but, rather, be embedded in subtle interactions among the thousands of factors considered.

A second risk is that, unlike traditional systems built on explicit logic rules, neural network systems deal with statistical truths rather than literal truths. That can make it difficult, if not impossible, to prove with complete certainty that the system will work in all cases—especially in situations that weren't represented in the training data. Lack of verifiability can be a concern in mission-critical applications, such as controlling a nuclear power plant, or when life-or-death decisions are involved.

Third, when the ML system does make errors, as it almost inevitably will, diagnosing and correcting exactly what's going wrong can be difficult. The underlying structure that led to the solution can be unimaginably complex, and the solution may be far from optimal if the conditions under which the system was trained change.

While all these risks are very real, the appropriate benchmark is not perfection but the best available alternative. After all, we humans, too, have biases, make mistakes, and have trouble explaining truthfully how we arrived at a particular decision. The advantage of machine-based systems is that they can be improved over time and will give consistent answers when presented with the same data.

Does that mean there is no limit to what artificial intelligence and machine learning can do? Perception and cognition cover a great deal of territory—from driving a car to forecasting sales to deciding whom to hire or promote. We believe the chances are excellent that AI will soon reach superhuman levels of performance in most or all of these areas. So what *won't* AI and ML be able to do?

We sometimes hear "Artificial intelligence will never be good at assessing emotional, crafty, sly, inconsistent human beings—it's too rigid and impersonal for that." We don't agree. ML systems like those at Affectiva are already at or beyond human-level performance in discerning a person's emotional state on the basis of tone of voice or facial expression. Other systems can infer when even the world's best poker players are bluffing well enough to beat them at the amazingly complex game Heads-Up No-Limit Texas Hold'em. Reading people accurately is subtle work, but it's not magic. It requires perception and cognition—exactly the areas in which ML is currently strong and getting stronger all the time.

A great place to start a discussion of the limits of AI is with Pablo Picasso's observation about computers: "But they are useless. They can only give you answers." They're actually far from useless, as ML's recent triumphs show, but Picasso's observation still provides insight. Computers are devices for answering questions, not for posing them. That means entrepreneurs, innovators, scientists, creators, and other kinds of people who figure out what problem or opportunity to tackle next, or what new territory to explore, will continue to be essential.

Similarly, there's a huge difference between passively assessing someone's mental state or morale and actively working to change it. ML systems are getting quite good at the former but remain well behind us at the latter. We humans are a deeply social species; other humans, not machines, are best at tapping into social drives such as compassion, pride, solidarity, and shame in order to persuade, motivate, and inspire. In 2014 the TED Conference and the XPRIZE Foundation announced an award for "the first artificial intelligence to come to this stage and give a TED Talk compelling enough to win a standing ovation from the audience." We doubt the award will be claimed anytime soon.

We think the biggest and most important opportunities for human smarts in this new age of superpowerful ML lie at the intersection of two areas: figuring out what problems to work on next, and persuading a lot of people to tackle them and go along with the solutions. This is a decent definition of leadership, which is becoming much more important in the second machine age.

The status quo of dividing up work between minds and machines is falling apart very quickly. Companies that stick with it are going to find themselves at an ever-greater competitive disadvantage compared with rivals who are willing and able to put ML to use in all the places where it is appropriate and who can figure out how to effectively integrate its capabilities with humanity's.

A time of tectonic change in the business world has begun, brought on by technological progress. As was the case with steam power and electricity, it's not access to the new technologies themselves, or even to the best technologists, that separates winners from losers. Instead, it's innovators who are open-minded enough to see past the status quo and envision very different approaches, and savvy enough to put them into place. One of machine learning's greatest legacies may well be the creation of a new generation of business leaders.

In our view, artificial intelligence, especially machine learning, is the most important general-purpose technology of our era. The impact of these innovations on business and the economy will be reflected not only in their direct contributions but also in their ability to enable and inspire complementary innovations. New products and processes are being made possible by better vision systems, speech recognition, intelligent problem solving, and many other capabilities that machine learning delivers.

Some experts have gone even further. Gil Pratt, who now heads the Toyota Research Institute, has compared the current wave of AI technology to the Cambrian explosion 500 million years ago that birthed a tremendous variety of new life forms. Then as now, one of the key new capabilities was vision. When animals first gained this capability, it allowed them to explore the environment far more effectively; that catalyzed an enormous increase in the number of species, both predators and prey, and in the range of ecological niches that were filled. Today as well we expect to see a variety of new products, services, processes, and organizational forms and also numerous extinctions. There will certainly be some weird failures along with unexpected successes.

Although it is hard to predict exactly which companies will dominate in the new environment, a general principle is clear: The most nimble and adaptable companies and executives will thrive. Organizations that can rapidly sense and respond to opportunities will seize the advantage in the AI-enabled landscape. So the successful strategy is to be willing to experiment and learn quickly. If managers aren't ramping up experiments in the area of machine learning, they aren't doing their job. Over the next decade, AI won't replace managers, but managers who use AI will replace those who don't.

The most important new general-purpose technology is artificial intelligence, particularly machine learning. ML systems are replacing older algorithms in many applications and are now superior at many tasks previously done best by humans.

✓ Machine learning is fundamentally different from the software that preceded it: The machine learns from examples, rather than being explicitly programmed for a particular outcome.

✓ Organizations looking to put ML to use should be aware that AI skills are spreading quickly; the necessary algorithms and hardware for modern AI can be bought or rented as needed; and they may not need much data to start using ML productively.

✓ ML systems have low "interpretability," meaning that humans have difficulty figuring out how the systems reach their decisions. This creates three risks: The machines may have hidden biases; it is often impossible to prove that an ML system will work in all mission-critical situations; and when the ML system does make errors, diagnosing the problem and correcting it can be difficult.

✓ Companies that continue to divide up work between minds and machines will increasingly lose their competitive advantage to rivals that effectively integrate AI's capabilities with human capabilities.

Adapted from content posted on hbr.org, August 7, 2017 (product #BG1704).

2

INSIDE FACEBOOK'S AI WORKSHOP

An interview with Joaquin Candela by Scott Berinato

Within Facebook's cavernous Building 20, about halfway between the lobby (panoramic views of the Ravenswood Slough) and the kitchen (hot breakfast, smoothies, gourmet coffee), in a small conference room called Lollapalooza, Joaquin Candela is trying to explain artificial intelligence to a layperson.

Candela—bald, compact, thoughtful—runs Facebook's Applied Machine Learning (AML) group, the engine room of AI at Facebook, which increasingly makes it the engine room of Facebook in general. After some verbal searching, he finally says:

Look, a machine learning algorithm really is a lookup table, right? Where the key is the input, like an image, and the value is the label for the input, like "a horse." I have a bunch of examples of something. Pictures of horses. I give the algorithm as many as I can. "This is a horse. This is a horse. This isn't a horse. This is a horse." And the algorithm keeps those in a table. Then, if a new example comes along—or if I tell it to watch for new examples— well, the algorithm just goes and looks at all those examples we fed it. Which rows in the table look similar? And how similar? It's trying to decide, "Is this new thing a horse? I think so." If it's right, the image gets put in the "This is a horse" group, and if it's wrong, it gets put in the "This isn't a horse" group. Next time, it has more data to look up.

One challenge is how do we decide how similar a new picture is to the ones stored in the table. One aspect of machine learning is to learn similarity functions. Another challenge is, What happens when your table grows really large? For every new image, you would need to make a zillion comparisons . . . So another aspect of machine learning is to approximate a large stored table with a function instead of going through every image. The function knows how to roughly estimate what the cor-

*responding value should be. That's the essence of
machine learning—to approximate a gigantic table
with a function. This is what learning is about.*

There's more to it than that, obviously, but it's a good
starting point when talking about AI because it makes it
sound real, almost boring. Mechanical. So much of the
conversation around AI is awash in mystical descriptions
of its power and in reverence for its near-magic capabilities. Candela doesn't like that and tries to use more-prosaic
terms. It's powerful, yes, but not magical. It has limitations.
During presentations, he's fond of showing a slide with
a wizard and a factory, telling audiences that Facebook
thinks of AI like the latter, because "wizards don't scale."

And that's what Facebook has done with AI and machine learning: scaled it at a breakneck pace. A few years
ago the company's machine learning group numbered
just a few and needed days to run an experiment. Now,
Candela says, several hundred employees run thousands
of experiments a day. AI is woven so intricately into
the platform that it would be impossible to separate the
products—your feed, your chat, your kid's finsta—from
the algorithms. Nearly everything users see and do is in-
formed by AI and machine learning.

Understanding how and why Facebook has so fully
embraced AI can help any organization that's ready to

invest in an algorithmic future. It would be easy to assume that Facebook, with all its resources, would simply get the best talent and write the best algorithms—game over. But Candela took a different approach. Certainly the talent is strong, and the algorithms are good. Some of them are designed to "see" images or automatically filter them. Some understand conversations and can respond to them. Some translate between languages. Some try to predict what you'll like and buy.

But in some ways the algorithms are not his main focus. Instead, he's been busy creating an AI workshop in which anyone in the company can use AI to achieve a goal. Basically, Candela built an AI platform for the platform. Whether you're a deeply knowledgeable programmer or a complete newbie, you can take advantage of his wares.

Here's how he did it and what you can learn from it.

Soyuz

Candela, a veteran of Microsoft Research, arrived at Facebook in 2012 to work in the company's ads business. He and a handful of staffers inherited a ranking algorithm for better targeting users with ads.

Candela describes the machine learning code he inherited as "robust but not the latest." More than once he compares it to Soyuz, the 1960s Soviet spacecraft. Basic but reliable. Gets the job done even if it's not the newest, best thing. "It'll get you up there and down. But it's not the latest covnet [convolutional neural net] of the month."

You might assume, then, that the first thing Candela set out to do was to upgrade the algorithm. Get rid of Soyuz in favor of a space plane. It wasn't. "To get more value, I can do three things," he says. "I can improve the algorithm itself, make it more sophisticated. I can throw more and better data at the algorithm so that the existing code produces better results. And I can change the speed of experimentation to get more results faster.

"We focused on data and speed, not on a better algorithm."

Candela describes this decision as "dramatic" and "hard." Computer scientists, especially academic-minded ones, are rewarded for inventing new algorithms or improving existing ones. A better statistical model is the goal. Getting cited in a journal is validation. Wowing your peers gives you cred.

It requires a shift in thinking to get those engineers to focus on business impact before optimal statistical model. He thinks many companies are making the mistake of structuring their efforts around building the best algorithms, or hiring developers who claim to have the best algorithms, because that's how many AI developers think.

But for a company, a good algorithm that improves the business is more valuable than vanguard statistical models. In truth, Candela says, real algorithmic breakthroughs are few and far between—two or three a year at best. If his team focused its energies there, it would take lots of effort to make marginal gains.

He hammers these points home constantly: Figure out the impact on the business first. Know what you're solving for. Know what business challenge you need to address. "You might look for the shiniest algorithm or the people who are telling you they have the most advanced algorithm. And you really should be looking for people who are most obsessed with getting any algorithm to do a job. That's kind of a profound thing that I think is lost in a lot of the conversation. I had a conversation with our resident machine learning geek at our office, and we were just talking about different people doing AI. He said, 'Nobody really thinks their algorithms are very good or whatever.' It makes me think, maybe that's fine.

"I'm not saying don't work on the algorithm at all. I'm saying that focusing on giving it more data and better data, and then experimenting faster, makes a lot more sense."

So rather than defining success as building the best natural language processing algorithm, he defines it as deploying one that will help users find a restaurant when they ask their friends, "Where can I get a good bite around here?" Instead of being thrilled that some computer vision algorithm is nearing pixel-perfect object recognition, he gets excited if that AI is good enough to notice that you post a lot of pictures of the beach and can help you buy a swimsuit.

The strategy worked when he started at Facebook. Ad revenues rose. Candela's profile rose. It was suggested that AML become a centralized function for all of Facebook. Candela said no. Twice. "I was concerned about the 'If you build it, they will come' phenomenon." Just creating bits of artificial intelligence in the hope that people would see the value and adopt it wouldn't work.

But he did pick his spots. He collaborated with the feeds team while saying no to many other groups. Then he worked with the Messenger team. His team grew and took on more projects with other teams.

By 2015 Candela could see that his group would need to centralize, so he turned his attention to how he'd build such an operation. He was still worried about the "build it and they will come" phenomenon, so he focused less on how his team would be structured and more on how the group would connect to the rest of Facebook. "You build a factory that makes amazing widgets, and you forget to design the loading docks into your factory?" He laughs. "Well, enjoy your widgets."

Only then, about three years in, did Candela think about upgrading some of his algorithms. (Incidentally, even today, the emergency escape spacecraft attached to the International Space Station is a Soyuz.)

H2

Candela goes to a whiteboard to describe how he built his AI factory inside Facebook. The key, he says, was figuring out where on the product development path AI fits. He draws something like the graph in figure 2-1.

H3—Horizon 3, or three years out from product—is the realm of R&D and science. Often, data scientists who

FIGURE 2-1

Where AI fits in at Facebook

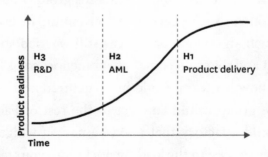

Source: Facebook

work on AI think of themselves as here, improving algorithms and looking for new ways to get machines to learn. Candela didn't put his team here for the reasons already mentioned. It's too far from impact on the business. H1, approaching product delivery, is where the product teams live—the feeds team, the Instagram team, the ads team. AI doesn't go here either, because it would be difficult to retrofit products this deeply developed. It would be like building a car and then deciding that it should be self-driving after you started to put it together.

That leaves H2, between the science and the product, as the place AML lives at Facebook. AML is a conduit for transferring the science into the product. It does not do research for research's sake, and it does not build and ship products. As the upward slope in the product's readiness shows, it's a dynamic space. Pointing to H2, Candela says, "This needs to feel uncomfortable all the time. The people you need to hire need to be okay with that, and they need to be incredibly selfless. Because if your work is successful, you spin it out. And you need to fail quite a bit. I'm comfortable with a 50% failure rate."

If the team is failing less, Candela suspects its members are too risk averse, or they're taking on challenges that are sliding them closer to H1's product focus. "Maybe we do something like that and it works, but it's still a failure, because the product teams should be taking that on, not us. If you own a piece of technology that the ads team should operate themselves to generate value, give it to them, and then increase your level of ambition in the machine learning space before something becomes product."

So Candela's team is neither earning the glory of inventing new statistical models nor putting products out into the world. It's a factory of specialists who translate others' science for others' products and fail half the time.

Push/Pull

All that being said, the lines between the three realms—H3, H2, and H1—still aren't crisp. In some cases Candela's team does look at the science of machine learning to solve specific problems. And sometimes it does help build the products.

That was especially true as AML got off the ground, because many people in the business hadn't yet been exposed to AI and what it could do for them. In one case AML built a translation algorithm. The team dipped into the research space to look at how existing translation algorithms worked and could be improved, because bad translations, which either don't make sense or create a misleading interpretation, are in some ways worse than no translation.

"Early on it was more push, more tenacity on our part," Candela says. "But it was gentle tenacity. We weren't going to throw something over the fence and tell the product team, 'This is great, use it.'" That meant that his team helped write some product code. Doing a little bit of the science and a little bit of the product in addition to its core function was meant to inspire the product team members to see what AML could do for them.

What the two teams built—a product that allowed community pages to instantly translate into several languages—worked. Other projects were similarly pushed out, and now the international team and other product groups at Facebook are pulling from AML, asking to use code in their products themselves.

"Look, it's nowhere near where I want it to be," Candela says. "I'd like to have all the product leaders in the company get together quarterly for AI reviews. That will certainly happen. But the conversation in the past two years has completely changed. Now if I walk from one end of this building to the other and I bump into, I don't know, the video team or the Messenger team, they'll stop me and say, 'Hey, we're excited to try this. We think we can build a product on this.' That didn't happen before."

AML's success, though, has created a new challenge for Candela. Now that everyone wants a piece of AML, the factory has to scale.

Layer Cake

Candela couldn't scale just by saying yes to every project and adding bodies to get the work done. So he organized in other ways. First he subdivided his team according to the type of AI its members would focus on (see figure 2-2).

This created common denominators so that one team—say, computer vision—could work on any machine learning application involving parsing images and reuse its work whenever possible.

Next came a large-scale engineering effort to build Facebook's own AI backbone, called FBLearner Flow. Here algorithms are deployed once and made reusable for anyone who may need them. The time-consuming parts of setting up and running experiments are automated, and past results are stored and made available and easily searchable. And the system runs through a serious hardware array, so many experiments can be run simultaneously. (The system allows for more than 6 million predictions a second.) All of this is to increase the velocity of running experiments on the data and scale.

The system was also designed to accommodate many kinds of possible users. Candela believes that for AI to work, and to scale even further, he must help people

FIGURE 2-2

Applied machine learning

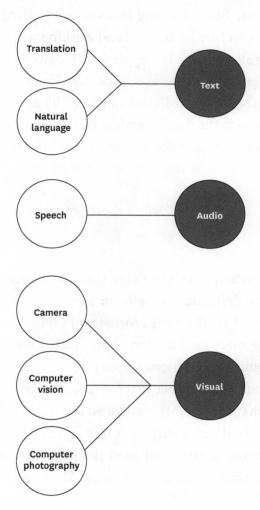

Source: Facebook

outside AML do the work themselves. He created what he calls a layer cake of artificial intelligence (see figure 2-3).

The bottom layers focus on AML's work: refining the core engine (with a strong focus on optimizing performance, especially for mobile) and working with machine learning algorithms. The upper layers focus on tools that make it possible for those outside AML to exploit the algorithms with less AML involvement. "It's all about what you expose to the user," Candela says. In some cases he's built systems that developers outside AML can take advantage of to build and run their own models.

Rex

A good example of Candela's team structure and the push/pull dynamic comes from some AI built to surface content on the basis of what you type. The natural-language machine learning team created an engine to understand conversational typing.

This bit of intelligence first found its way into the Messenger chat client. AML developed the models while the product team developed use cases and "intents"—lingo for the types of tasks you want the engine to learn. For example, training natural language AI to recognize and

FIGURE 2-3

Layer cake of AI

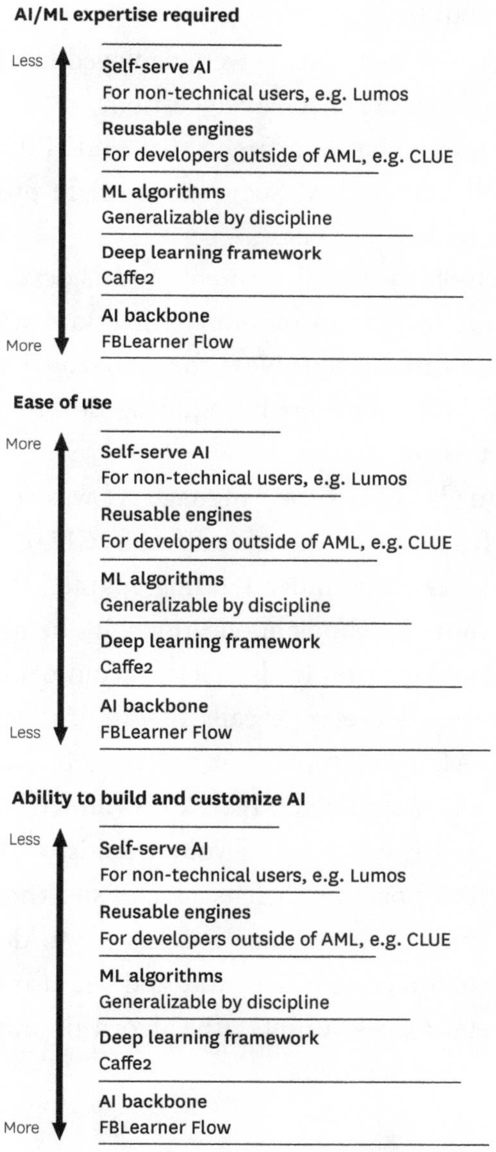

AI/ML expertise required

Less ↑

More ↓

Self-serve AI
For non-technical users, e.g. Lumos

Reusable engines
For developers outside of AML, e.g. CLUE

ML algorithms
Generalizable by discipline

Deep learning framework
Caffe2

AI backbone
FBLearner Flow

Ease of use

More ↑

Less ↓

Self-serve AI
For non-technical users, e.g. Lumos

Reusable engines
For developers outside of AML, e.g. CLUE

ML algorithms
Generalizable by discipline

Deep learning framework
Caffe2

AI backbone
FBLearner Flow

Ability to build and customize AI

Less ↑

More ↓

Self-serve AI
For non-technical users, e.g. Lumos

Reusable engines
For developers outside of AML, e.g. CLUE

ML algorithms
Generalizable by discipline

Deep learning framework
Caffe2

AI backbone
FBLearner Flow

Source: Facebook

reliably respond to a phrase like "I'm looking for the best . . ." is an intent.

The first few such intents were deployed to Messenger through a product called M Suggestions.

If you sent a chat to a friend that said "I'll meet you there in 30 minutes," M Suggestions might prompt you with an offer to hire a car.

As the tools for building intent models developed and the product team became more conversant with them, AML's role diminished. Now the Messenger team has improved M Suggestions by building dozens more intents on its own.

Still, this bit of natural language AI wasn't built just for chat. It's reusable. It was codified as CLUE, for "conversational learning understanding engine." It found its way into more Facebook applications. It's being adapted for status updates and feeds. Social recommendations— or social rex, as everyone calls them—are increasingly driven by AI. If you typed "I'm traveling to Omaha and I really want to find a good steak downtown," AI might respond as if it were one of your friends, with a comment on your post, rex such as a list of steakhouses, and a tagged map of where they are relative to downtown. If your friend replied to you and said, "It also has some great vegetarian restaurants," the algorithm might again reply with pertinent data.

Social rex intents are not yet being developed without AML, but the goal is to have them move out of Candela's group, just as M Suggestions did.

In general, the idea is to make product teams AI-capable themselves. "We'll teach you to fish," Candela says, "and you go fish, and we'll drag up the next thing. We'll build a fishing boat. And once you're using the fishing boat, I'm going to build a cannery, right?"

At the moment, about 70% of the AI work on the backbone is done by people outside Candela's team. That's possible in part because of the interface with AI. In some cases, as with a tool called Lumos, machine learning can be used by nondevelopers.

Horseback Riding and Cereal Boxes

Lumos is computer vision AI, a tool that can comb through photos on Facebook or Instagram or other platforms and learn what they contain. You can train it to see anything. It has helped automate the discovery and banning of pornographic or violent content, IP appropriation (improper use of brands and logos), and other unwelcome content. It can also help identify things you like and do (to drive personalized advertising and recommendations) on the basis of photos in your feeds.

I watch a demo in which engineers select "horseback riding" as our intent, the thing we'll be looking for. The interface is simple: A few clicks, a couple of forms to fill out—What are you looking for? How much data do you want to look at?—and the algorithm gets to work finding pictures of horseback riding. Thumbnails start to fill the page.

The algorithm has searched for horseback riding before, so it's already quite good at finding it. My guess is that north of 80% of the images that pop up are indeed of horseback riding, and they show remarkable variety. Here's one with someone posing at a standstill. Here's one with the horse rearing. Here's an equestrian jumping. The algorithm finds shapes and boundaries between shapes and builds on previous knowledge of what those interactions mean. It knows things about what combination of pixels is most likely a person, for example, and what's a horse. It knows when it "sees" a person and a horse together with the person situated close above the horse. And it decides that this looks like horseback riding.

We also find pictures that aren't horseback riding—one is a person standing next to a horse; another is a person on a mule—and check those off as not matches. They're framed in red, in case there's any doubt. The algorithm internalizes that information—adds it to the lookup table—for use next time. A simple chart at the top of the page shows the algorithm's accuracy and confidence over time. It's always an S curve, slow to learn at first, then rapidly improving, then tapering off on how much more accurate it can get. It's very good at seeing horseback riding.

Other potentially valuable pictures are harder for AI to parse. "Receipts" is tricky to suss out because it can look to a computer just like type on a page; but there would be some interesting apps for AI that could recognize and "read" receipts. The engineers show how bowling alleys and escalators often confuse the algorithm because they have similar shapes and visual properties.

I ask, "What about something like 'food'?" This brings us to an important point about machine learning: It's only as good as its training.

We call up food as a topic to train. Indeed, we see lots of pictures of fruits and vegetables, a few of plates at restaurants. All food. We also see a cereal box. Is that food?

Well, yes. Or no. It's a box. But there's food in it. When we buy it, we're buying food, not the box. If I asked if there was any food in the cupboard, you wouldn't say, "No, just a cereal box." (Or, more pertinent to Facebook, if I posted a picture of a cereal box, should it think I'm posting about food or about a box?) As a picture, as a piece of data, it's a box.

Should we mark this as a match or a miss? Here's part of the art of machine learning. When training algorithms, one needs to use clearly definable categories. Food is probably too general in some ways, and the algorithm will either improperly hit or miss on images because it's hard to know what we mean when we say "Show me pictures of food." "Vegetable" is a better idea to train on. And when training, everyone must define terms in the same way. Imagine two people training the algorithm when one always marks cereal boxes as food and the other marks them as not food. Now imagine that happening at scale, on terabytes of visual data.

The same applies to natural language processing. Humans are very good at interpreting text in context to find sophisticated meaning. For example, I may type, "Gee, I love that movie about the superheroes. It's so, so original! I hope they make a hundred more of them." My friends, who know me and know some of the mechanics of sarcasm, may readily understand that my meaning is the opposite of what I'm typing. Artificial intelligence is still learning how to decide the meaning of something like that. To figure out if I'm being sarcastic, it has to go much further than just learning how to parse grammar and vocabulary. It has to see what else I've said and posted and try to find other clues that will tell it whether I really loved the movie and I want 100 more or I actually detested it—because getting that wrong is not good for a platform that wants to create affinities with me.

If I was being sarcastic and my feed starts filling up with superhero movie ads, I'm probably not enjoying the experience.

Not Magic

It's details like these—showing where AI is still limited, how humans have such a core role in training it, and how solving problems and creating value are more important than finding great models—that Candela is thinking about near the end of the day, when he's talking about the mythic status AI has gained. He's railing against what he perceives as laziness in those who find the idea of AI-as-magic-bullet appealing and don't apply critical thinking to it.

"What frustrates me," he says, "is that everybody knows what a statistician is and what a data analyst can do. If I want to know 'Hey, what age segment behaves in what way?' I get the data analyst.

"So when people skip that, and they come to us and say, 'Hey, give me a machine learning algorithm that will do what we do,' I'm like, 'What is it that I look like? What problem are you trying to solve? What's your goal? What are the trade-offs?'" Sometimes they're surprised that there are trade-offs. "If that person doesn't have answers to those questions, I'm thinking, 'What the hell are you thinking AI is?'"

They are thinking it's magic.

"But it's not. That's the part where I tell people, 'You don't need machine learning. You need to build a data science team that helps you think through a problem and apply the human litmus test. Sit with them. Look at your data. If you can't tell what's going on, if you don't have any intuition, if you can't build a very simple, rule-based system—like, *Hey, if a person is younger than 20 and living in this geography, then do this thing*—if you can't do that, then I'm extremely nervous even talking about throwing AI at your problem.'

"I'm delighted when other executives come to me and start not from wanting to understand the technology but from a problem they have that they've thought very, very deeply about. And sometimes—often, in fact—a simple, good old rule-based system, if you have the right data, will get you 80% of the way to solving the problem.

"And guess what? It's going to have the benefit that everybody understands it. Exhaust the human brain first."

TAKEAWAYS

In Facebook's Applied Machine Learning (AML) group, several hundred employees run thousands of experiments a day. Understanding how and why Facebook has so fully embraced AI can help any organization that's ready to invest in an algorithmic future.

✓ Knowing what business challenge you need to address should be more important to your company than trying to make technological breakthroughs. A basic but reliable algorithm that improves the business is more valuable than pioneering vanguard statistical models.

✓ Facebook thinks of three horizons for developing and deploying AI capabilities. The first is existing products—if these products aren't already driven by AI, they won't have AI retrofitted onto them. The second is AML, between science and product, a factory of specialists that translates others' science for others' products and still fails half the time. The third horizon, three years out from product delivery, is the realm of R&D and data scientists.

✓ AI shouldn't be used for every data or prediction problem. Often, a simple, rule-based system will solve the problem if you have the right data.

Adapted from content posted on hbr.org, July 19, 2017 (product #BG1704).

3

WHY COMPANIES THAT WAIT TO ADOPT AI MAY NEVER CATCH UP

by Vikram Mahidhar and Thomas H. Davenport

While some companies—most large banks, Ford and GM, Pfizer, and virtually all tech firms—are aggressively adopting artificial intelligence, many are not. Instead they are waiting for the technology to mature and for expertise in AI to become more widely available. They are planning to be "fast followers"—a strategy that has worked with most information technologies.

We think this is a bad idea. It's true that some technologies need further development, but some (like traditional machine learning) are quite mature and have been available in some form for decades. Even more recent technologies like deep learning are based on research that took place in the 1980s. New research is being conducted all the time, but the mathematical and statistical foundations of current AI are well established.

System Development Time

Beyond the technical maturity issue, there are several other problems with the idea that companies will be able to adopt quickly once technologies are more capable. First, there is the time required to develop AI systems. Such systems will probably add little value to your business if they are completely generic, so time is required to tailor and configure them to your business and the specific knowledge domain within it. If the AI you are adopting employs machine learning, you will have to round up a substantial amount of training data. If it manipulates language—as in natural language processing applications—it can be even more difficult to get systems up and running. There is a lot of taxonomy and local knowledge that needs to be incorporated into the AI system—similar to the old "knowledge engineering" activity for expert systems. AI of this type is not just a software coding problem; it is a knowledge coding problem. It takes time to discover, disambiguate, and deploy knowledge.

If your knowledge domain has not already been modeled by your vendor or consultant, it will typically require many months to design. This is particularly true for complex knowledge domains. For example, Memorial Sloan Kettering Cancer Center has been working with IBM to use Watson to treat certain forms of cancer for over six years, and the system still isn't ready for broad use despite availability of high-quality talent in cancer care and AI. There are several domains and business problems for which the requisite knowledge engineering is available. However, it still needs to be manipulated to a company's specific business context.

Integration Time

Even once your systems have been built, there is the issue of integrating AI systems into your organization. Unless you are employing some AI capabilities that are embedded within existing packaged application systems that your company already uses (for example, Salesforce Einstein features within your CRM system), the fit with your business processes and IT architecture will require significant planning and time for adaptation. The transition from pilots and prototypes to production systems for AI can be difficult and time-consuming.

Even if your organization is skilled at moving pilots and prototypes into production, you will also have to re-engineer the business processes to have full impact on your business and industry. In most cases AI supports individual tasks and not entire business processes, so you will have to redesign business processes and new human tasks around it. If you want to affect customer engagement, for example, you will need to develop or adapt multiple AI applications and tasks that relate to different aspects of marketing, sales, and service relationships.

Human Interactions with AI Time

Finally, there are the human challenges of AI to overcome. Very few AI systems are fully autonomous but rather are focused on augmentation of and by human workers. New AI systems typically mean new roles and skills for the humans who work alongside them, and it will typically require considerable time to retrain workers on the new process and system. For example, investment advice companies providing "robo-advice" to their customers have often attempted to get human advisers to shift their focus to "behavioral finance," or providing advice and "nudges" to encourage wise decisions and actions in investing. But this sort of skill is quite different from providing advice about what stocks and bonds to buy and will take some time to inculcate.

Even if the goal for an AI system is to be fully autonomous, it is likely that some period of time in augmentation mode will be necessary. During this period, a critical piece of machine learning occurs through interaction between the system and its human users and observers. Called *interaction learning*, this is a critical step for organizations to understand how the system interacts with its ecosystem. They can often gather new data sets and begin to bake them into algorithms during this period—which often takes months or years.

Governance Time for AI Applications

While AI systems are geared to provide exponential scale and predictions, they will need a much broader governing approach than the classic controls- and testing-driven approach. The efficacy of AI algorithms decays over time because these are built based on historical data and recent business knowledge. The algorithms can be updated as the machine learns from patterns in new data, but they will need to be monitored by subject-matter experts to ensure the machine is interpreting the change in business context correctly. Algorithms will also have to be continuously monitored for bias. For instance, if an AI system is trained to create product recommendations based on customer demographics and the demographics change dramatically in new data, it may provide biased recommendations.

Governance will also include watching for customer fraud. As the systems become smart, so will the users. They may try to game the systems with fraudulent data and activities. Monitoring and preventing this will require sophisticated instrumentation and human monitoring in the context of your business.

Winners Take All

It may, then, take a long time to develop and fully implement AI systems, and there are few if any shortcuts to the necessary steps. Once they have been successfully undertaken, scaling—particularly if the company has a plentiful supply of data and the knowledge engineering mastered—can be very rapid. By the time a late adopter has done all the necessary preparation, earlier adopters will have taken considerable market share—they'll be able to operate at substantially lower costs with better performance. In short, the winners may take all and late adopters may never catch up. Think, for example, of the learning and capability that a company like Pfizer—which has, according to one of the leaders of the company's Analytics and AI Lab, more than 150 AI projects underway—has already accumulated. Tech companies like Alphabet have even more learning; that company had 2,700 AI projects underway as far back as 2015.

Admittedly, some steps can be accelerated by waiting, if a company is willing to compromise its unique knowledge and ways of conducting business. Vendors are developing a vast variety of knowledge graphs and models that use techniques ranging from natural language processing to computer vision. If one exists for your industry or business problem, and you're willing to adopt it with little modification, that will speed up the process of AI adoption. But you may lose your distinctive competence or competitive advantage if you do not tweak it to fit your context and build everything around it.

The obvious implication is that if you want to be successful with AI and think there may be a threat from AI-driven competitors or new entrants, you should start learning now about how to adapt it to your business across multiple different applications and AI methods. Some leading companies have created a centralized AI group to do this at scale. Such central groups focus on framing the problems, proving out the business hypothesis, modularizing the AI assets for reusability, creating techniques to manage the data pipeline, and training across businesses. One other possibility may be to acquire a startup that has accumulated substantial AI capabilities, but there will still be the need to adapt those capabilities to your business. In short, you should get started now if you haven't already, and hope that it's not too late.

Many companies are waiting for AI technology to mature before adopting it—using a "fast follower" approach—but there are several problems with this plan.

- ✓ Systems developed by a vendor or consultant will probably add little value to your business if they are completely generic. You'll need time to tailor and configure them to your business.

- ✓ Even once your systems are built, the transition from pilots and prototypes to production systems for AI can be difficult, and you will also have to reengineer certain business processes for AI systems to have their full impact.

✓ New AI systems typically mean new roles and skills for the humans who work alongside them. This will require considerable, time-consuming retraining for workers on the new processes and systems.

✓ By the time a fast follower has done the necessary preparation, earlier adopters will have taken considerable market share, operating at lower cost with better performance. The winners may take all—and late adopters may never catch up.

Adapted from content posted on hbr.org, December 6, 2018 (product #H04OK4).

Section 2

ADOPTING AI

4

THREE QUESTIONS ABOUT AI THAT NONTECHNICAL EMPLOYEES SHOULD BE ABLE TO ANSWER

by Emma Martinho-Truswell

A rticles about artificial intelligence often begin with an intention to shock readers, referencing classic works of science fiction or alarming statistics about impending job losses. But I think we get closer to the heart of AI when we think about small and mundane ways in which AI makes work just a little easier. And it's not necessarily the AI experts in your organization who will identify these mundane problems that AI can help solve. Instead, employees throughout the organization will be able to spot the low-hanging fruit where AI could make your organization more efficient, but only if they know what AI is capable of doing, and what it should never do.

For example, I manage the finances for a team that travels very often, and I've been grateful for the intelligent guesswork that my expenses software extracts from receipts using machine learning: the merchant's name, the dollar amount spent, taxes, and likely expense categorization. Finding opportunities for this kind of clever improvement, saving human time and energy, is not just a leadership challenge. It's a search best undertaken by as many people within the organization as possible.

A fast-growing area of artificial intelligence is machine learning, in which a computer program improves its answers to a question by creating and iterating algorithms based on data. It is often regarded as the kind of technology that only the cleverest and most mathematically minded people can understand and work with. Indeed, those who work day to day building machine learning programs will tend to have postgraduate degrees in computer science. But machine learning is a technological tool like any other: It can be understood on various levels and can still be used by those whose understanding is incomplete. People do not need to know how to fly a plane to be able to spot sensible new airline routes. Instead, they need to know approximately what a plane can and cannot do. For instance, laypeople might also have ideas about what planes should *not* be used for, which could result in positive outcomes such as reducing aircraft noise in the middle of cities or limiting costly flights for very short journeys.

When leaders in companies, nonprofits, or governments invest in artificial intelligence, much of their attention goes to hiring machine learning experts, or paying for tools. But this misses a critical opportunity. For organizations to get the most that they can from AI, they should also be investing in helping all of their team members to understand the technology better. Understanding machine learning can make an employee more likely to spot potential applications in her own work. Many of the most promising uses for machine learning will be humdrum, and this is where technology can be at its most useful: saving people time, so that they can concentrate on the many tasks at which they outperform machines. An executive assistant who has a better understanding of machine learning might suggest that calendar software learn more explicitly from patterns that develop over time, reminding him when his boss has not met with a team member for an unusually long time. A calendar that learns patterns could give an executive assistant more time for the human specialties of his job, such as helping his boss to manage a team.

So, what *should* all of your employees be learning about AI? There are three important questions that any member of your team should be able to answer: How does artificial intelligence work? What is it good at? And what should it never do? Let's look at each in more detail.

How Does It Work?

Team members who aren't responsible for building an AI system should nonetheless know how it processes information and answers questions. It's particularly important for people to understand the differences between how they learn and how a machine "learns." For example, a human trying to analyze one million data points will need to simplify it in some way in order to make sense of it—perhaps by finding an average or creating a chart. A machine learning algorithm, on the other hand, can use every individual data point when it makes its calculations. It is "trained" to spot patterns using an existing set of data inputs and outputs. Because data is fundamental to a machine's ability to provide useful answers, a manager should ensure that her team members have some basic data literacy. This means helping people to understand what numbers are telling us, and the biases and errors that might be hidden within them. Understanding data—the fuel of AI—helps people to understand what AI is good at.

What Is It Good At?

Machine learning tools excel when they can be trained to solve a problem using vast quantities of reliable data, and to give answers within clear parameters that people have defined for them. My expenses software is a perfect example: It has the receipts of its millions of users to learn from, and it uses them to help predict whether a cup of coffee from Starbucks should be categorized as travel, stationery, or entertainment. Learning what machine learning is good at quickly helps someone to see what machine learning is *not* good at. Problems that are novel, or which lack meaningful data to explain them, remain squarely in the realm of human specialties. Help your employees to understand this difference by showing them tools they already use that are powered by AI, either within the organization or outside it (such as social media advertising or streaming service recommendations). These examples will help team members to understand AI's enormous potential, but also its limitations.

What Should It Never Do?

Just because machine learning can solve a problem does not mean it should do so. A machine cannot understand, for example, the biases that data reveals, nor the consequences of the advice it gives. There may be some problems that your organization should never ask an AI application to solve. For example, I would not want an algorithm to make the final decision in my company on whom to hire, what to discuss at a board meeting, or how to manage a poorly performing staff member. If employees have thought about the proper ethical limitations of AI, they can be important guards against its misuse.

The organizations that will do best in the age of artificial intelligence will be good at finding opportunities for AI to help employees do their day-to-day jobs better and will be able to implement those ideas quickly. They will be clear about where to deploy machine learning, and where to avoid it. Alongside their investments in technology, they will remind their teams of the importance of human specialties: supporting colleagues, communicating well, and experimenting with novel ideas. To be ready for pervasive AI, an organization's whole team will need to be ready too.

TAKEAWAYS

Employees throughout your company may be able to spot the low-hanging fruit where AI could make your organization more efficient, but only if they have some minimum knowledge of AI. Any member of your team should be able to answer the following questions:

✓ **How does it work?** Team members who aren't responsible for building an AI system should nonetheless know how it processes information and answers questions. Understanding data—the fuel of AI—helps people understand what AI is good at.

✓ **What is it good at?** Machine learning tools excel when they can be trained to solve a problem using vast quantities of reliable data, and to give answers within clear parameters that people have defined for them. Help your employees understand this difference by showing them tools they already use that are powered by AI, either within the organization or outside it.

✓ **What should it never do?** Just because machine learning *can* solve a problem does not mean it should. If employees understand the ethical limitations of AI, they can be important guards against its misuse.

Adapted from content posted on hbr.org, August 2, 2018 (product #H04GEB).

5

IS YOUR COMPANY'S DATA ACTUALLY VALUABLE IN THE AI ERA?

by Ajay Agrawal, Joshua Gans, and Avi Goldfarb

Artificial intelligence is coming. That's what we've heard over the past few years, and what we'll continue to hear over the next few. For established businesses that are not Google or Facebook, a natural question to ask is: What have we got that is going to allow us to survive this transition?

In our experience, when business leaders ask this with respect to AI, the answer they are given is "data." This view is confirmed by the business press. There are hundreds of articles claiming that "data is the new oil"—by which they mean it is a fuel that will drive the AI economy.

If that is the case, then your company can consider itself lucky. You collected all this data, and then it turned out you were sitting on an oil reserve when AI happened to show up. But when you have that sort of luck, it is probably a good idea to ask, "Are we really that lucky?"

The "data is oil" analogy does have some truth to it. Like internal combustion engines with oil, AI needs data to run. AI takes in raw data and converts it into something useful for decision making. Want to know the weather tomorrow? Let's use data on past weather. Want to know yogurt sales next week? Let's use data on past yogurt sales. AIs are prediction machines driven by data.

But does AI need *your* data? There is a tendency these days to see all data as potentially valuable for AI, but that isn't really the case. Yes, data, like oil, is used day to day to operate your prediction machine. But the data you are sitting on now is likely not that data. Instead, the data you have now, which your company accumulated over time, is the type of data used to *build* the prediction machine—not operate it.

The data you have now is training data. You use that data as input to train an algorithm. And you use that algorithm to generate predictions to inform actions.

So, yes, that does mean your data is valuable. But it does not mean your business can survive the storm. Once your data is used to train a prediction machine, it is devalued. It is not useful anymore for that sort of prediction. And there are only so many predictions your data will be useful for. To continue the oil analogy, data can be burned. It is somewhat lost after use. Scientists know this. They spend years collecting data, but once it has produced research findings, it sits unused in a file drawer or on a backup disk. Your business may be sitting on an oil well, but it's finite. It doesn't guarantee you more in the AI economy than perhaps a more favorable liquidation value.

Even to the extent that your data could be valuable, your ability to capture that value may be limited. How many other sources of comparable data exist? If you are one of many yogurt vendors, then your database containing the past 10 years of yogurt sales and related data (price, temperature, sales of related products like ice cream) will have less market value than if you are the only owner of that type of data. In other words, just as with oil, the greater the number of other suppliers of your type of data, the less value you can capture from your training data. The value of your training data is further influenced by the value generated through enhanced prediction accuracy. Your training data is more valuable if enhanced prediction accuracy can increase yogurt sales by $100 million rather than only $10 million.

Moreover, the ongoing value of data usually comes from the actions you take in your day-to-day business—the new data you accrue each day. New data allows you to *operate* your prediction machine after it is trained. It also enables you to improve your prediction machine through *learning*. While 10 years of data on past yogurt sales is valuable for training an AI model to predict future yogurt sales, the actual predictions used to manage the supply chain require operational data on an ongoing basis. And this is the important point for today's incumbent companies.

An AI startup that acquires a trove of data on past yogurt sales can train an AI model to predict future sales. It can't actually use its model to make decisions unless the startup obtains ongoing operational data to learn from. Unlike startups, large enterprises generate operational data every day. That's an asset. The more operations, the more data. Furthermore, the owner of the operation can actually make use of the prediction. It can use the prediction to enhance its future operation.

In the AI economy, the value of your accumulated data is limited to a onetime benefit from training your AI model. And the value of training data is, like oil or any other input, influenced by the overall supply—it's less valuable when more people have it. In contrast, the value of your ongoing operational data is not limited to a onetime benefit, but rather provides a perpetual benefit for operating and further enhancing your prediction machine. So, despite all the talk about data being the new oil, your accumulated historical data isn't the thing. However, it may be the thing that *gets you to* the thing. Its value for your future business prospects is low. But if you can find ways to generate a new, ongoing data stream that delivers a performance advantage in terms of your AI's predictive power, that will give you sustainable leverage when AI arrives.

TAKEAWAYS

It is conventional wisdom that companies that are sitting on troves of data enjoy great advantages as they transition to the AI-driven economy. But many leaders don't realize that the data they have is what they need to *build* AI systems, not to operate them and gain new insights from them.

✓ Even when your data is useful, your ability to capture value from it may be limited. If your competitors have compiled similar data sets, your data won't allow you to make predictions any better than theirs will.

✓ Fully trained AI models must be fed ongoing operational data to make predictions that have business value. Large companies have an advantage because they generate large sets of operational data every day.

✓ Only companies that have both data to train their AI models and ongoing data streams to make predictions that have business value will be able to leverage AI for sustainable advantage.

Adapted from content posted on hbr.org, January 17, 2018 (product #H04421).

6

HOW TO CHOOSE YOUR FIRST AI PROJECT

by Andrew Ng

A rtificial intelligence is poised to transform every industry, just as electricity did 100 years ago. It will create $13 trillion of GDP growth by 2030, according to McKinsey, most of which will be in non-internet sectors including manufacturing, agriculture, energy, logistics, and education. The rise of AI presents an opportunity for executives in every industry to differentiate and defend their businesses. But implementing a companywide AI strategy is challenging, especially for legacy enterprises.

My advice for executives, in any industry, is to start small. The first step to building an AI strategy, drawn from my article the "AI Transformation Playbook," is to choose one to two company-level pilot AI projects.[1] These projects will help your company gain momentum and gain firsthand knowledge of what it takes to build an AI product.

Five Traits of a Strong AI Pilot Project

Tapping the power of AI technologies requires customizing them to your business context. The purpose of your one or two pilot projects is only partly to create value; more importantly, the success of these first projects will help convince stakeholders to invest in building up your company's AI capabilities.

When you're considering a pilot AI project, ask yourself the following questions:

1. Does the project give you a quick win?

Use your first AI pilot project to get the flywheel turning as soon as possible. Choose initial projects that can be done quickly (ideally within 6 to 12 months) and have a high chance of success. Instead of doing only one pilot project, choose two to three to increase the odds of creating at least one significant success.

2. Is the project either too trivial or too unwieldy in size?

Your pilot project does not have to be the most valuable AI application, as long as it delivers a quick win. But it should be meaningful enough so that a success convinces other company leaders to invest in further AI projects.

In the early days of leading the Google Brain team, I faced widespread skepticism within Google about the potential of deep learning. Speech recognition was much less important to Google than web search and advertising, so I had my team take on speech as our first internal customer. By helping the speech team build a much more accurate recognition system, we convinced other teams to have faith in Google Brain. For our second project, we worked with Google Maps to increase data quality. Each successful project increased the momentum in the flywheel, and Google Brain played a leading role in turning Google into the great AI company it is today.

3. Is your project specific to your industry?

By choosing a company-specific project, your internal stakeholders can directly understand the value. For example, if you run a medical devices company, building an AI + Recruiting project to automatically screen résumés is a bad idea for two reasons: (1) There's a high chance someone else will build an AI + Recruiting platform that serves a much larger user base and will outperform what you could do in-house and/or will undercut you; (2) This project is less likely to convince the rest of your company that AI is worth investing in than if your pilot project applied AI to medical devices. It is more valuable to build a health-care-specific AI system—anything ranging from using AI to assist doctors with crafting treatment plans, to streamlining the hospital check-in process through automation, to offering personalized health advice.

4. Are you accelerating your pilot project with credible partners?

If you are still building up your AI team, consider working with external partners to bring in AI expertise quickly.

Eventually, you will want to have your own in-house AI team; however, waiting to build a team before executing might be too slow relative to the pace of AI's rise.

5. Is your project creating value?

Most AI projects create AI value in one of three ways: reducing costs (automation creates opportunities for cost reduction in almost every industry), increasing revenue (recommendation and prediction systems increase sales and efficiency), or launching new lines of business (AI enables new projects that were not possible before).

You can create value even without having big data, which is often overhyped. Some businesses, such as web search, have a long tail of queries, and so search engines with more data do perform better. However, not all businesses have this amount of data, and it may be possible to build a valuable AI system with perhaps as few as 100–1,000 data records (though more does not hurt). Do not choose projects just because you have a lot of data in industry X and believe the AI team will figure out how to turn this data into value. Projects like this tend to fail. It is important to develop a thesis upfront about how specifically an AI system will create value.

Setting Up Your AI Project for Success

So what do these traits look like in practice?

AI is automation on steroids. A rich source of ideas for AI projects will lie in automating tasks that humans are doing today, using a technology called supervised learning. You will find that AI is good at automating *tasks*, rather than *jobs*. Try to identify the specific tasks that people are doing and examine if any can be automated. For example, the tasks involved in a radiologist's job may include reading X-rays, operating imaging machinery, consulting with colleagues, and planning surgery. Rather than trying to automate their entire *job*, consider if just one of the *tasks* could be automated or made faster through partial automation.

Before executing on an AI pilot, I recommend clearly stating the desired timeline and outcome, and allocating a reasonable budget to the team.

Appoint a leader

Choose someone who can work cross-functionally and bridge both AI and your industry's domain experts. This will ensure that when the project succeeds, it will influence the rest of the organization. Their goal is *not* to build an AI startup. Their goal is to build a successful project that will influence the rest of the company's beliefs and state of knowledge about AI as a first step toward building future projects.

Conduct business value *and* technical diligence

Make sure that, if executed successfully, the business leaders agree that this project will create sufficient value for the business. But also make sure that the project is feasible. Technical diligence can take a few weeks, requiring a technical team to examine what data you have and perhaps even carry out small-scale experiments.

Build a small team

I have seen numerous pilot ideas that were executed with about 5 to 15 people. The exact level of resources varies wildly per project, but scoping projects that can be done with a small team ensures that everyone can know everyone else and work cross-functionally, and perhaps also makes the allocation of resources more painless. While there are some projects today that require 100+ (or even

1,000+) engineers to do well, such a high level of resourcing is likely not necessary for your pilot AI project.

Communicate

When the pilot project hits key milestones, and especially when it delivers a successful result, be sure to give the team an internal platform—ranging from talks, to awards, to even external PR—to allow their work to become known inside the company. Making sure the project team is recognized by the CEO and is visibly successful will be a key part to building momentum. If you have an AI technology team working with a business team, make sure also that the business team receives plenty of credit and rewards for the success. This will encourage other business teams to jump into AI as well.

Having led Google Brain and Baidu's AI Group, which were respectively leading forces for turning Google and Baidu into great AI companies, I think most companies can and should become good at AI. Your goal should not be to compete with the leading internet companies, but rather to master AI for your vertical industry sector. And remember: The first step is to select the right pilot projects and execute on them.

TAKEAWAYS

The first step to building an AI strategy is to choose one to two company-level pilot projects. These initiatives will help your company gain momentum and gain firsthand knowledge of what it takes to build an AI product.

✓ When you're considering a pilot AI project, ask yourself the following five questions:

1. Does the project give you a quick win?

2. Is the project either too trivial or too unwieldy in size?

3. Is the project specific to your industry?

4. Are you accelerating your pilot project with credible partners?

5. Is your project creating value?

✓ Before executing on an AI pilot, leaders should clearly state the desired timeline and outcome, allocate a reasonable budget, appoint a team leader who can bridge between AI and your industry's domain experts, conduct business value and technical due diligence, and build a small team.

✓ When the pilot project hits key milestones, and especially when it delivers a positive result, the team should communicate the success to others in the company.

NOTE

1. Andrew Ng, "AI Transformation Playbook" (working paper, Landing AI, 2018), https://landing.ai/content/uploads/2018/12/AI -Transformation-Playbook-v8.pdf.

Adapted from content posted on hbr.org, February 6, 2019 (product #H04S3S).

7

WHAT WILL HAPPEN WHEN YOUR COMPANY'S ALGORITHMS GO WRONG?

by Roman V. Yampolskiy

When you're ready to incorporate artificial intelligence technologies in your business, the analysis you should perform is this: What can possibly go wrong? What is our product or service expected to do? What happens if it fails to do so? Do we have a damage mitigation plan? Consider the embarrassing situation that Microsoft found itself in with its Tay chatbot fiasco, where internet trolls exploited vulnerabilities in the bot's code, feeding it racist, homophobic, and sexist content that millions read on social media.

Accidents, including deadly ones, caused by software or industrial robots can be traced to the early days of such technology, but they are not necessarily caused by the systems themselves. AI failures, on the other hand, are directly related to the mistakes produced by the intelligence such systems are designed to exhibit. We can broadly classify such failures into "mistakes made during the learning phase" and "mistakes made during performance phase." A system can fail to learn what its designers want it to learn and might instead learn a different, but correlated function.

A frequently cited example is a computer vision system that the U.S. Army had hoped to use to automatically detect camouflaged enemy tanks. The system was supposed to classify pictures of tanks, but instead learned to distinguish the backgrounds of such images. Other examples include problems caused by poorly designed functions that would reward AIs for only partially desirable behaviors, such as pausing a game to avoid losing, or repeatedly touching a soccer ball to get credit for possession.

It can help to look at some recent examples of AI failure to better understand what problems are likely to arise and what you can do to prevent them—or at least to clean up quickly after a failure. Consider these examples of AI failures from the past few years:[1]

- An automated email-reply generator created inappropriate responses, such as writing "I love you" to a business colleague.

- A robot for grabbing auto parts grabbed and killed a man.

- Image-tagging software classified black people as gorillas.

- Medical AI classified patients with asthma as having a lower risk of dying of pneumonia.

- Adult-content-filtering software failed to remove inappropriate content, exposing children to violent and sexual content.

- AI designed to predict recidivism acted racist.

- An AI agent exploited a reward signal to win a game without actually completing the game.

- Video game NPCs (nonplayer characters, or any character that is not controlled by a human player) designed unauthorized superweapons.

- AI judged a beauty contest and rated dark-skinned contestants lower.

- A mall security robot collided with and injured a child.

- A self-driving car had a deadly accident.

And every day, consumers experience more common shortcomings of AI: Spam filters block important emails, GPS provides faulty directions, machine translations corrupt the meaning of phrases, autocorrect replaces a desired word with a wrong one, biometric systems misrecognize people, transcription software fails to capture what is being said; overall, it is harder to find examples of AIs that *don't* fail.

Analyzing the list of AI failures, we can arrive at a simple generalization: An AI designed to do X will eventually fail to do X. While it may seem trivial, it is a powerful generalization tool, which can be used to predict future failures of AI. For example, looking at cutting-edge current and future AI, we can predict that:

- AI doctors will misdiagnose some patients in a way a real doctor would not.

- Video-description software will misunderstand movie plots.

- Software for generating jokes will occasionally fail to make them funny.

- Sarcasm-detection software will confuse sarcastic and sincere statements.

- Employee-screening software will be systematically biased and thus hire low performers.

- The Mars robot explorer will misjudge its environment and fall into a crater.

- Tax-preparation software will miss important deductions or make inappropriate ones.

What should you learn from these examples and analysis? Failures will happen! It's inevitable. But we can still put best practices in place, such as:

- Controlling user input to the system and limiting learning to verified data inputs

- Checking for racial, gender, age, and other common biases in your algorithms

- Explicitly analyzing how your software can fail, and then providing a safety mechanism for each possible failure

- Having a less "smart" backup product or service available

- Having a communications plan in place to address the media in case of an embarrassing failure (Hint: Start with an apology.)

I predict that both the frequency and seriousness of AI failures will steadily increase as AIs become more capable. The failures of today's narrow domain AIs are just the tip of the iceberg; once we develop general artificial intelligence capable of cross-domain performance, embarrassment will be the least of our concerns.

TAKEAWAYS

There are countless examples of an AI designed for a task eventually failing to do that task. As AI performs more consequential functions, damage caused by single failures will become more severe.

✓ When your business is ready to incorporate AI technologies, perform this risk analysis: What can possibly go wrong with our AI? What is our product or service expected to do? What happens if it fails to do so? Do we have a damage mitigation plan?

✓ To mitigate damage from AI failures, companies should follow these best practices:

- Control user input into system and only use verified data.

- Check for racial, gender, age, and other common biases in algorithms.

- Analyze how the software can fail, and then provide a safety mechanism for each possible failure.

- Have a less "smart" backup product or service available.

- Have a communications plan in place to address the media in case of an embarrassing failure.

NOTE

1. Bálint Miklós, "Computer, Respond to This Email: Introducing Smart Reply in Inbox by Gmail," The Key Word (Google), November 3, 2015, https://blog.google/products/gmail/computer-respond-to-this-email/; Eliana Dockterman, "Robot Kills Man at Volkswagen Plant," Time, July 2, 2015, http://time.com/3944181/robot-kills-man-volkswagen-plant/; Taryn Finley, "Google Apologizes for Tagging Photos of Black People as 'Gorillas,'" Huffington Post, July 2, 2015, https://www.huffingtonpost.com/2015/07/02/google

-black-people-goril_n_7717008.html; Rich Caruana et al., "Intelligible Models for HealthCare: Predicting Pneumonia Risk and Hospital 30-Day Readmission," Proceedings of the 21th ACM SIGKDD International Conference on Knowledge Discovery and Data Mining, August 10, 2015, http://people.dbmi.columbia.edu /noemie/papers/15kdd.pdf; Alistair Barr, "Google's YouTube Kids App Criticized for 'Inappropriate Content,'" *Wall Street Journal*, May 19, 2015, https://blogs.wsj.com/digits/2015/05/19/googles -youtube-kids-app-criticized-for-inappropriate-content/; Andy Cush, "This Program That Judges Use to Predict the Future Seems Racist as Hell," *Gawker*, May 23, 2016, https://gawker.com/this -program-that-judges-use-to-predict-future-crimes-s-1778151070; Jack Dario, "Faulty Reward Functions in the Wild," OpenAI Blog, December 21, 2016, https://blog.openai.com/faulty-reward -functions/; Julian Benson, "Elite's AI Created Super Weapons and Started Hunting Players. Skynet Is Here," *Kotaku*, June 3, 2016, http://www.kotaku.co.uk/2016/06/03/elites-ai-created-super -weapons-and-started-hunting-players-skynet-is-here; Sam Levin, "A Beauty Contest Was Judged by AI and the Robots Didn't Like Dark Skin," *Guardian*, April 8, 2016, https://www.theguardian .com/technology/2016/sep/08/artificial-intelligence-beauty-contest -doesnt-like-black-people; Veronica Rocha, "Crime-Fighting Robot Hits, Rolls Over Child at Silicon Valley Mall," *LA Times*, July 14, 2016, https://www.latimes.com/local/lanow/la-me-ln-crimefighting -robot-hurts-child-bay-area-20160713-snap-story.html; Sam Levin and Nicky Woolf, "Tesla Driver Killed While Using Autopilot Was Watching Harry Potter, Witness Says," *Guardian*, July 1, 2016, https://www.theguardian.com/technology/2016/jul/01/tesla-driver -killed-autopilot-self-driving-car-harry-potter.

Adapted from content posted on hbr.org, April 10, 2017 (product #H03L3S).

Section 3

AI AND THE FUTURE OF WORK

8

HOW WILL AI CHANGE WORK?

Here Are Five Schools of Thought

by Mark Knickrehm

The future of the workforce is one of the biggest issues facing CEOs today. It's abundantly clear to all that artificial intelligence, big data analytics, and advanced robotics make it possible for machines to take on tasks that once required a person to do them. How should companies prepare, strategically, to thrive in this world?

Views on what to expect vary dramatically. By some accounts, almost half of all jobs in the U.S. economy could be made obsolete. Others have described how intelligent machines will actually create jobs—including entirely new categories of jobs. Some people even talk about a world of superabundance where work will be about pursuing your passion, on your own terms.

It's critical for companies to understand the range of opinions on this issue, because implicitly or explicitly, they will influence the way business leaders create the workforce of the future. And while a lot will shake out in years to come, this issue is already front and center. Companies are making decisions today that will matter hugely to their ability to compete tomorrow and throughout the 2020s.

Most companies are already moving rapidly to acquire new capabilities. In Accenture's "Reworking the Revolution" survey of 1,200 C-level executives worldwide, 75% say that they are currently accelerating investments in AI and other intelligent technologies. And 72% say they are responding to a competitive imperative—they recognize the need for new tools to keep up with rivals, both by improving productivity and by finding new sources of growth. Some companies are transforming themselves into "intelligent enterprises," in which all processes are digitized, decisions are data-driven, and machines do the heavy lifting—both physical and cognitive.

The author thanks his colleagues in Accenture Research, Svenja Falk, David Light, and Geoffrey Lewis, for their contributions to this article.

So, there's a great deal at stake in the debate over productivity and jobs. Leaders must understand the debate and be prepared to address tough questions: What kind of new skills do we need? How should we be organized? How do we define jobs? How can we bring our people along with us, in a way that benefits everyone?

Through research, we've identified five schools of thought in this debate.

The dystopians: Man and machine will wage a Darwinian struggle that machines will win. AI systems will take on tasks at the heart of middle- and high-skill jobs, while robots will perform menial work that requires low-skill labor. The result will be massive unemployment, falling wages, and wrenching economic dislocation. Falling incomes will have grave consequences in places like the United States and Europe, where consumption accounts for 56% or 69% of GDP, respectively, requiring new social supports, such as a universal basic income.

The utopians: Intelligent machines will take on even more work, but the result will be unprecedented wealth, not economic decline. AI and computing power will advance in the next two decades to achieve "the singularity"— when machines will be able to emulate the workings of the human brain in its entirety. Human brains will be scanned and downloaded to computers and billions of replicated human brains will do most of the cognitive work, while robots will do all the heavy lifting. Economic output could double every three months. The singularity may even lead to a world where little human labor is required, a universal income program covers basic needs, and people apply their talents to meaningful pursuits.

The technology optimists: A burst of productivity has already begun but is not captured in official data because companies are still learning how intelligent technologies can change how they operate. When companies do take full advantage of intelligent technologies, a leap in productivity will produce a digital bounty—creating both economic growth and improvements in living standards not counted in GDP, such as consumer surplus (from better, cheaper products) and the value of free apps and information. However, based on current trends, the bounty won't be distributed evenly, and many jobs will be displaced. To avoid negative income and employment effects, there will be a need to invest in education and training alongside investments in technology.

The productivity skeptics: Despite the power of intelligent technologies, any gains in national productivity levels will be low. Combine that with headwinds from aging populations, income inequality, and the costs of dealing with climate change, and the United States will have near-zero GDP growth. In the end, there isn't much to do except brace for stagnant growth in advanced economies.

The optimistic realists: Digitization and intelligent machines can spur productivity gains that match previous technology waves. Productivity will advance rapidly in certain sectors and for high-performing companies. New jobs will be created, but intelligent technologies may exacerbate the trends of the recent past, in which demand rose for both high- and low-skill workers whose jobs could be easily automated, while demand for middle-skill workers fell. With no simple solutions, more research is needed into the true relationship between productivity, employment, and wages to uncover effective responses.

Three Actions for Shaping the Future

Our crystal ball for what things might look like in 10 years is cloudy. What we do know is that business leaders must take steps now to shape their workforces for the emerging intelligent enterprise. Our research and experience point to three critical imperatives.

Use technology to augment human skills and reinvent operating models

Companies that think beyond labor substitution and cost savings will see a much greater payoff. For example, a new class of adaptive robots can function safely alongside workers and can take on difficult and tedious work. Consider this example: At BMW's Spartanburg, South Carolina, plant, robots are installing door-sealing gaskets, an awkward and tiring job for workers. This speeds up the line, improves quality, and gives workers more time to do higher-value work. Researchers estimate that using adaptive robots this way could cut time wasted on nonvalue-added work by 25%. Employee surveys show that workers have more positive views of the new robots, which they regard as useful helpers. Away from the factory, companies are using AI to offload routine work from employees and to give them new analytical tools to improve customer experience and discover new possibilities for products, services, and business models that drive growth.

Take the opportunity to redefine jobs and rethink organizational design

Companies cannot optimize their investments if they have the same old job descriptions and organizational structures. Executives should assess the tasks that need to be done, anticipate which ones will be transferred to machines, then reconfigure jobs by adding new tasks or creating entirely different roles that are needed for managing intelligent technologies. A factory worker, for example, can be trained to run robots. AI systems also need human help to train and correct algorithms and override fallible machine judgment. For example, at Stitch Fix, an online clothing subscription service, 3,400 human stylists work with an AI recommendation engine to make personalized suggestions for customers. The machines give stylists the speed they need to be productive, and the stylists provide the additional judgment needed for accurate recommendations (and fewer returns). To function effectively, an intelligent enterprise should have a nonhierarchical organization, in which employees collaborate across functional and operational silos. This enables the intelligent enterprise to act quickly on the insights from data-crunching machines and deploy human talent to swarm on problems, experiment, iterate, and get solutions into the market.

Make employees your partners in building the intelligent enterprise

To strike the right balance between investing in intelligent technologies and maintaining existing businesses, companies need help from their employees. In our (the previously referenced Accenture survey) research, we have found that employees are far more willing—even eager—to master new technologies than employers appreciate. They want to learn new skills, not least because they know they will need them to remain employed. Investments in both technology and training will help companies make a smooth transition to the intelligent enterprise. Companies that do this stand to outperform competitors because they will unleash the human talents that machines still can't match and that are essential to growth—creativity, empathy, communications, adaptability, and problem solving. "As basic automation and machine learning move toward becoming commodities," says Devin Fidler, research director at the Institute for the Future, "uniquely human skills will become more valuable."

The debate over technology and jobs will rage on. Business leaders must follow this debate—and participate in it, too. And much more research is needed to fully understand the implications of intelligent technologies for work. In the meantime, companies that actively seize control of what can be done to prepare will position themselves to thrive in this exciting new era.

TAKEAWAYS

Companies need to understand the varying opinions on how AI will change work and society, because implicitly or explicitly, these beliefs will influence the way they develop the workforce of the future.

✓ Five schools of thought are central to this debate:

- **Dystopians.** Man and machine will wage a Darwinian struggle that machines will win.

- **Utopians.** Intelligent machines will take on even more work, but the result will be unprecedented wealth, not economic decline.

- **Technology optimists.** A burst of productivity has already begun but is not captured in official data.

- **Productivity skeptics.** Despite the power of intelligent technologies, any productivity gains will be low.

- **Optimistic realists.** Digitization and intelligent machines can spur productivity gains that match previous technology waves.

✓ Executives who want to position their companies to thrive in the AI future should set the following goals:

- Use technology to augment human skills and reinvent operating models.

- Take the opportunity to redefine jobs and rethink organizational design.

- Make employees partners in building the intelligent enterprise.

Adapted from content posted on hbr.org, January 24, 2018 (product #H0449F).

9

COLLABORATIVE INTELLIGENCE

Humans and AI Are Joining Forces

by H. James Wilson and Paul Daugherty

Artificial intelligence is becoming good at many "human" jobs—diagnosing disease, translating languages, providing customer service—and it's improving fast. This is raising reasonable fears that AI will ultimately replace human workers throughout the economy. But that's not the inevitable, or even most likely, outcome. Never before have digital tools been so responsive to us, nor we to our tools. While AI will radically alter how work gets done and who does it, the technology's

The Value of Collaboration

Companies benefit from optimizing collaboration between humans and artificial intelligence. Five principles can help them do so: Reimagine business processes; embrace experimentation/employee involvement; actively direct AI strategy; responsibly collect data; and redesign work to incorporate AI and cultivate related employee skills. A survey of 1,075 companies in 12 industries found that the more of these principles companies adopted, the better their AI initiatives performed in terms of speed, cost savings, revenues, or other operational measures (see the figure).

larger impact will be in complementing and augmenting human capabilities, not replacing them.

Certainly, many companies have used AI to automate processes, but those that deploy it mainly to displace employees will see only short-term productivity gains. In our research involving 1,500 companies, we found that firms achieve the most significant performance improvements when humans and machines work together. Through such collaborative intelligence, humans and AI actively enhance each other's complementary strengths: the leadership, teamwork, creativity, and social skills of the former, and the speed, scalability, and quantitative

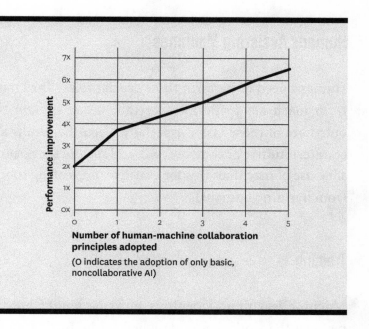

Number of human-machine collaboration principles adopted

(0 indicates the adoption of only basic, noncollaborative AI)

capabilities of the latter. What comes naturally to people (making a joke, for example) can be tricky for machines, and what's straightforward for machines (analyzing giga-bytes of data) remains virtually impossible for humans. Business requires both kinds of capabilities.

To take full advantage of this collaboration, companies must understand how humans can most effectively aug-ment machines, how machines can enhance what humans do best, and how to redesign business processes to support the partnership. Through our research and work in the field, we have developed guidelines to help companies achieve this and put the power of collaborative intelligence to work.

Humans Assisting Machines

Humans need to perform three crucial roles. They must *train* machines to perform certain tasks; *explain* the outcomes of those tasks, especially when the results are counterintuitive or controversial; and *sustain* the responsible use of machines (by, for example, preventing robots from harming humans).

Training

Machine learning algorithms must be taught how to perform the work they're designed to do. In that effort, huge training data sets are amassed to teach machine-translation apps to handle idiomatic expressions, medical apps to detect disease, and recommendation engines to support financial decision making. In addition, AI systems must be trained how best to interact with humans. While organizations across sectors are now in the early stages of filling trainer roles, leading tech companies and research groups already have mature training staffs and expertise.

Consider Microsoft's AI assistant, Cortana. The bot required extensive training to develop just the right personality: confident, caring, and helpful but not bossy.

Instilling those qualities took countless hours of attention by a team that included a poet, a novelist, and a playwright. Similarly, human trainers were needed to develop the personalities of Apple's Siri and Amazon's Alexa to ensure that they accurately reflected their companies' brands. Siri, for example, has just a touch of sassiness, as consumers might expect from Apple.

AI assistants are now being trained to display even more complex and subtle human traits, such as sympathy. The startup Koko, an offshoot of the MIT Media Lab, has developed technology that can help AI assistants seem to commiserate. For instance, if a user is having a bad day, the Koko system doesn't reply with a canned response such as "I'm sorry to hear that." Instead it may ask for more information and then offer advice to help the person see his issues in a different light. If he were feeling stressed, for instance, Koko might recommend thinking of that tension as a positive emotion that could be channeled into action.

Explaining

As AIs increasingly reach conclusions through processes that are opaque (the so-called black-box problem), they require human experts in the field to explain their behavior to nonexpert users. These "explainers" are particularly important in evidence-based industries, such as law and medicine, where a practitioner needs to understand how an AI weighed inputs into, say, a sentencing or medical recommendation. Explainers are similarly important in helping insurers and law enforcement understand why an autonomous car took actions that led to an accident—or failed to avoid one. And explainers are becoming integral in regulated industries—indeed, in any consumer-facing industry where a machine's output could be challenged as unfair, illegal, or just plain wrong. For instance, the European Union's new General Data Protection Regulation (GDPR) gives consumers the right to receive an explanation for any algorithm-based decision, such as the rate offer on a credit card or mortgage. This is one area where AI will contribute to *increased* employment: Experts estimate that companies will have to create about 75,000 new jobs to administer the GDPR requirements.

Sustaining

In addition to having people who can explain AI outcomes, companies need "sustainers"—employees who continually work to ensure that AI systems are functioning properly, safely, and responsibly.

For example, an array of experts, sometimes referred to as safety engineers, focuses on anticipating and trying to prevent harm by AIs. The developers of industrial robots that work alongside people have paid careful attention to ensuring that they recognize humans nearby and don't endanger them. These experts may also review analysis from explainers when AIs do cause harm, as when a self-driving car is involved in a fatal accident.

Other groups of sustainers make sure that AI systems uphold ethical norms. If an AI system for credit approval, for example, is found to be discriminating against people in certain groups (as has happened), these ethics managers are responsible for investigating and addressing the problem. Playing a similar role, data compliance officers try to ensure that the data that is feeding AI systems complies with the GDPR and other consumer-protection regulations. A related data-use role involves ensuring that AIs manage information responsibly. Like many tech companies, Apple uses AI to collect personal details about users as they engage with the company's devices and software. The aim is to improve the user experience, but unconstrained data gathering can compromise privacy, anger customers, and run afoul of the law. The company's "differential privacy team" works to make sure that while the AI seeks to learn as much as possible about a group of users in a statistical sense, it is protecting the privacy of individual users.

Machines Assisting Humans

Smart machines are helping humans expand their abilities in three ways. They can *amplify* our cognitive strengths; *interact* with customers and employees to free us for higher-level tasks; and *embody* human skills to extend our physical capabilities.

Amplifying

Artificial intelligence can boost our analytic and decision-making abilities by providing the right information at the right time. But it can also heighten creativity. Consider how Autodesk's Dreamcatcher AI enhances the imagination of even exceptional designers. A designer provides Dreamcatcher with criteria about the desired product—for example, a chair able to support up to 300 pounds, with a seat 18 inches off the ground, made of materials costing less than $75, and so on. She can also supply information about other chairs that she finds attractive. Dreamcatcher then churns out thousands of designs that match those criteria, often sparking ideas that the designer might not have initially considered. She can then guide the software, telling it which chairs she likes or doesn't, leading to a new round of designs.

Throughout the iterative process, Dreamcatcher performs the myriad calculations needed to ensure that each proposed design meets the specified criteria. This frees the designer to concentrate on deploying uniquely human strengths: professional judgment and aesthetic sensibilities.

Interacting

Human-machine collaboration enables companies to interact with employees and customers in novel, more effective ways. AI agents like Cortana, for example, can facilitate communications between people or on behalf of people, such as by transcribing a meeting and distributing a voice-searchable version to those who couldn't attend. Such applications are inherently scalable—a single chatbot, for instance, can provide routine customer service to large numbers of people simultaneously, wherever they may be.

SEB, a major Swedish bank, now uses a virtual assistant called Aida to interact with millions of customers. Able to handle natural-language conversations, Aida has access to vast stores of data and can answer many frequently asked questions, such as how to open an account or make cross-border payments. She can also ask callers follow-up questions to solve their problems, and she's able to analyze a caller's tone of voice (frustrated versus appreciative, for instance) and use that information to provide better service later. Whenever the system can't resolve an issue—which happens in about 30% of cases—it turns the caller over to a human customer-service representative and then monitors that interaction to learn how to resolve similar problems in the future. With Aida handling basic requests, human reps can concentrate on addressing more-complex issues, especially those from unhappy callers who might require extra handholding.

Embodying

Many AIs, like Aida and Cortana, exist principally as digital entities, but in other applications the intelligence is embodied in a robot that augments a human worker. With their sophisticated sensors, motors, and actuators, AI-enabled machines can now recognize people and objects and work safely alongside humans in factories, warehouses, and laboratories.

In manufacturing, for example, robots are evolving from potentially dangerous and "dumb" industrial machines into smart, context-aware "cobots." A cobot arm might, for example, handle repetitive actions that require heavy lifting, while a person performs complementary tasks that require dexterity and human judgment, such as assembling a gear motor.

Hyundai is extending the cobot concept with exoskeletons. These wearable robotic devices, which adapt to the user and location in real time, will enable industrial workers to perform their jobs with superhuman endurance and strength.

Reimagining Your Business

In order to get the most value from AI, operations need to be redesigned. To do this, companies must first discover and describe an operational area that can be improved. It might be a balky internal process (such as HR's slowness to fill staff positions), or it could be a previously intractable problem that can now be addressed using AI (such as quickly identifying adverse drug reactions across patient populations). Moreover, a number of new AI and advanced analytic techniques can help surface previously invisible problems that are amenable to AI solutions.

Next, companies must develop a solution through co-creation—having stakeholders envision how they might collaborate with AI systems to improve a process. Consider the case of a large agricultural company that wanted to deploy AI technology to help farmers. An enormous amount

Revealing Invisible Problems

Former U.S. Defense Secretary Donald Rumsfeld once famously distinguished among "known knowns," "known unknowns," and "unknown unknowns"—things you're not even aware you don't know. Some companies are now using AI to uncover unknown unknowns in their businesses. Case in point: GNS Healthcare applies machine learning software to find overlooked relationships among data in patients' health records and elsewhere. After identifying a relationship, the software churns out numerous hypotheses to explain it and then suggests which of those are the most likely. This approach enabled GNS to uncover a new drug interaction hidden in unstructured patient notes. CEO Colin Hill points out that this is not garden-variety data mining to find associations. "Our machine learning platform is not just about seeing patterns and correlations in data," he says. "It's about actually discovering causal links."

of data was available about soil properties, weather patterns, historical harvests, and so forth, and the initial plan was to build an AI application that would more accurately predict future crop yields. But in discussions with farmers, the company learned of a more pressing need. What farmers really wanted was a system that could provide real-time recommendations on how to increase productivity—which crops to plant, where to grow them, how much nitrogen to use in the soil, and so on. The company developed an AI system to provide such advice, and the initial outcomes were promising; farmers were happy about the crop yields obtained with the AI's guidance. Results from that initial test were then fed back into the system to refine the algorithms used. As with the discovery step, new AI and analytic techniques can assist in co-creation by suggesting novel approaches to improving processes.

The third step for companies is to scale and then sustain the proposed solution. SEB, for example, originally deployed a version of Aida internally to assist 15,000 bank employees but thereafter rolled out the chatbot to its one million customers.

Through our work with hundreds of companies, we have identified five characteristics of business processes that companies typically want to improve: flexibility, speed, scale, decision making, and personalization. When reimagining a business process, determine which of these characteristics is central to the desired transformation, how intelligent collaboration could be harnessed to address it, and what alignments and trade-offs with other process characteristics will be necessary.

Flexibility

For Mercedes-Benz executives, inflexible processes presented a growing challenge. Increasingly, the company's most profitable customers had been demanding individualized S-class sedans, but the automaker's assembly systems couldn't deliver the customization people wanted.

Traditionally, car manufacturing has been a rigid process with automated steps executed by "dumb" robots. To improve flexibility, Mercedes replaced some of those robots with AI-enabled cobots and redesigned its processes around human-machine collaborations. At the company's plant near Stuttgart, Germany, cobot arms guided by human workers pick up and place heavy parts, becoming an extension of the worker's body. This system puts the worker in control of the building of each car, doing less manual labor and more of a "piloting" job with the robot.

The company's human-machine teams can adapt on the fly. In the plant, the cobots can be reprogrammed easily with a tablet, allowing them to handle different tasks depending on changes in the workflow. Such agility has enabled the manufacturer to achieve unprecedented levels of customization. Mercedes can individualize vehicle production according to the real-time choices consumers make at dealerships, changing everything from a vehicle's dashboard components to the seat leather to the tire valve caps. As a result, no two cars rolling off the assembly line at the Stuttgart plant are the same.

Speed

For some business activities, the premium is on speed. One such operation is the detection of credit-card fraud. Companies have just seconds to determine whether they should approve a given transaction. If it's fraudulent, they will most likely have to eat that loss. But if they deny a legitimate transaction, they lose the fee from that purchase and anger the customer.

Like most major banks, HSBC has developed an AI-based solution that improves the speed and accuracy of fraud detection. The AI monitors and scores millions of transactions daily, using data on purchase location and customer behavior, IP addresses, and other information to identify subtle patterns that signal possible fraud. HSBC first implemented the system in the United States, significantly reducing the rate of undetected fraud and false positives, and then rolled it out in the United Kingdom and Asia. A different AI system used by Danske

TABLE 9-1

Enhancing performance

At organizations in all kinds of industries, humans and AI are collaborating to improve five elements of business processes.

Element	Business process	Company or organization	Type of collaboration
Flexibility	Auto manufacturing	Mercedes-Benz	Assembly robots work safely alongside humans to customize cars in real time.
	Product design	Autodesk	Software suggests new product design concepts as a designer changes parameters such as materials, cost, and performance requirements.
	Software development	Gigster	AI helps analyze any type of software project, no matter the size or complexity, enabling humans to quickly estimate the work required, organize experts, and adapt workflows in real time.
Speed	Fraud detection	HSBC	AI screens credit- and debit-card transactions to instantly approve legitimate ones while flagging questionable ones for humans to evaluate.
	Cancer treatment	Roche	AI aggregates patient data from disparate IT systems, speeding collaboration among specialists.
	Public safety	Singapore government	Video analytics during public events predicts crowd behavior, helping responders address security incidents rapidly.
Scale	Recruiting	Unilever	Automated applicant screening dramatically expands the pool of qualified candidates for hiring managers to evaluate.

Element	Business process	Company or organization	Type of collaboration
Scale (continued)	Customer service	Virgin Trains	Bot responds to basic customer requests, doubling the volume handled and freeing humans to address more-complex issues.
	Casino management	GGH Morowitz	Computer-vision system helps humans continuously monitor every gaming table in a casino.
Decision making	Equipment maintenance	General Electric	"Digital twins" and Predix diagnostic application provide techs with tailored recommendations for machine maintenance.
	Financial services	Morgan Stanley	Robo-advisers offer clients a range of investment options based on real-time market information.
	Disease prediction	Icahn School of Medicine at Mount Sinai	Deep Patient system helps doctors predict patients' risk of specific disease, allowing preventive intervention.
Personalization	Guest experience	Carnival Corporation	Wearable AI device streamlines the logistics of cruise-ship activities and anticipates guest preferences, facilitating tailored staff support.
	Health care	Pfizer	Wearable sensors for Parkinson's patients track symptoms 24/7, allowing customized treatment.
	Retail fashion	Stitch Fix	AI analyzes customer data to advise human stylists, who give customers individualized clothing and styling recommendations.

Bank improved its fraud-detection rate by 50% and decreased false positives by 60%. The reduction in the number of false positives frees investigators to concentrate their efforts on equivocal transactions the AI has flagged, where human judgment is needed.

The fight against financial fraud is like an arms race: Better detection leads to more-devious criminals, which leads to better detection, which continues the cycle. Thus, the algorithms and scoring models for combating fraud have a very short shelf life and require continual updating. In addition, different countries and regions use different models. For these reasons, legions of data analysts, IT professionals, and experts in financial fraud are needed at the interface between humans and machines to keep the software a step ahead of the criminals.

Scale

For many business processes, poor scalability is the primary obstacle to improvement. That's particularly true of processes that depend on intensive human labor with minimal machine assistance. Consider, for instance, the employee recruitment process at Unilever. The consumer goods giant was looking for a way to diversify its 170,000-person workforce. HR determined that it needed to focus on entry-level hires and then fast-track the best into management. But the company's existing processes weren't able to evaluate potential recruits in sufficient numbers—while giving each applicant individual attention—to ensure a diverse population of exceptional talent.

Here's how Unilever combined human and AI capabilities to scale individualized hiring: In the first round of the application process, candidates are asked to play online games that help assess traits such as risk aversion. These games have no right or wrong answers, but they help Unilever's AI figure out which individuals might be best suited for a particular position. In the next round, applicants are asked to submit a video in which they answer questions designed for the specific position they're interested in. Their responses are analyzed by an AI system that considers not just what they say but also their body language and tone. The best candidates from that round, as judged by the AI, are then invited to Unilever for in-person interviews, after which humans make the final hiring decisions.

It's too early to tell whether the new recruiting process has resulted in better employees. The company has been closely tracking the success of those hires, but more data is still needed. It is clear, however, that the new system has greatly broadened the scale of Unilever's recruiting. In part because job seekers can easily access the system by smartphone, the number of applicants doubled to 30,000 within a year, the number of universities represented surged from 840 to 2,600, and the socioeconomic diversity of new hires increased. Furthermore, the average time from application to hiring decision has dropped from four months to just four weeks, while the time that recruiters spend reviewing applications has fallen by 75%.

Decision making

By providing employees with tailored information and guidance, AI can help them reach better decisions. This can be especially valuable for workers in the trenches, where making the right call can have a huge impact on the bottom line.

Consider the way in which equipment maintenance is being improved with the use of "digital twins"—virtual models of physical equipment. General Electric builds such software models of its turbines and other industrial products and continually updates them with operating data streaming from the equipment. By collecting readings from large numbers of machines in the field, GE has amassed a wealth of information on normal and aberrant performance. Its Predix application, which uses machine learning algorithms, can now predict when a specific part in an individual machine might fail.

This technology has fundamentally changed the decision-intensive process of maintaining industrial equipment. Predix might, for example, identify some unexpected rotor wear and tear in a turbine, check the turbine's operational history, report that the damage has increased fourfold over the past few months, and warn that if nothing is done, the rotor will lose an estimated 70% of its useful life. The system can then suggest appropriate actions, taking into account the machine's current condition, the operating environment, and aggregated data about similar damage and repairs to other machines. Along with its recommendations, Predix can generate information about their costs and financial benefits and provide a confidence level (say, 95%) for the assumptions used in its analysis.

Without Predix, workers would be lucky to catch the rotor damage on a routine maintenance check. It's possible that it would go undetected until the rotor failed, resulting in a costly shutdown. With Predix, maintenance workers are alerted to potential problems before they become serious, and they have the needed information at their fingertips to make good decisions—ones that can sometimes save GE millions of dollars.

Personalization

Providing customers with individually tailored brand experiences is the holy grail of marketing. With AI, such personalization can now be achieved with previously unimaginable precision and at vast scale. Think of the way the music streaming service Pandora uses AI algorithms to generate personalized playlists for each of its millions of users according to their preferences in songs, artists, and genres. Or consider Starbucks, which, with customers' permission, uses AI to recognize their mobile devices and call up their ordering history to help baristas make serving recommendations. The AI technology does what it does best, sifting through and processing copious amounts of data to recommend certain offerings or actions, and humans do what they do best, exercising their intuition and judgment to make a recommendation or select the best fit from a set of choices.

The Carnival Corporation is applying AI to personalize the cruise experience for millions of vacationers through a wearable device called the Ocean Medallion and a network that allows smart devices to connect. Machine learning dynamically processes the data flowing from the medallion and from sensors and systems throughout the ship to help guests get the most out of their vacations.

The medallion streamlines the boarding and debarking processes, tracks the guests' activities, simplifies purchasing by connecting their credit cards to the device, and acts as a room key. It also connects to a system that anticipates guests' preferences, helping crew members deliver personalized service to each guest by suggesting tailored itineraries of activities and dining experiences.

The Need for New Roles and Talent

Reimagining a business process involves more than the implementation of AI technology; it also requires a significant commitment to developing employees with what we call "fusion skills"—those that enable them to work effectively at the human-machine interface. To start, people must learn to delegate tasks to the new technology, as when physicians trust computers to help read X-rays and MRIs. Employees should also know how to combine their distinctive human skills with those of a smart machine to get a better outcome than either could achieve alone, as in robot-assisted surgery. Workers must be able to teach intelligent agents new skills and undergo training to work well within AI-enhanced processes. For example, they must know how best to put questions to an AI agent to get the information they need. And there must be employees, like those on Apple's differential privacy team, who ensure that their companies' AI systems are used responsibly and not for illegal or unethical purposes.

We expect that in the future, company roles will be redesigned around the desired outcomes of reimagined processes, and corporations will increasingly be organized around different types of skills rather than around rigid job titles. AT&T has already begun that transition as it shifts from landline telephone services to mobile networks and starts to retrain 100,000 employees for new positions. As part of that effort, the company has completely overhauled its organizational chart: Approximately 2,000 job titles have been streamlined into a much smaller number of broad categories encompassing similar skills. Some of those skills are what one might expect (for example, proficiency in data science and data wrangling), while others are less obvious (for instance, the ability to use simple machine learning tools to cross-sell services).

Conclusion

Most activities at the human-machine interface require people to *do new and different things* (such as train a chatbot) and to *do things differently* (use that chatbot to provide better customer service). So far, however, only a small number of the companies we've surveyed have begun to reimagine their business processes to optimize collaborative intelligence. But the lesson is clear: Organizations that use machines merely to displace workers through automation will miss the full potential of AI. Such a strategy is misguided from the get-go. Tomorrow's leaders will instead be those that embrace collaborative intelligence, transforming their operations, their markets, their industries, and—no less important—their workforces.

TAKEAWAYS

AI is having the most significant impact—and companies are seeing the biggest performance gains—when it augments human workers instead of replacing them. To take full advantage, companies must understand how humans and machines can work together, and how to redesign business processes to support the partnership.

✓ Humans need to perform three crucial roles to help augment machines: *train* machines to perform certain tasks, *explain* the outcomes of those tasks, and *sustain* the responsible use of machines.

✓ Smart machines are helping humans enhance their abilities by *amplifying* our cognitive strengths; *interacting* with customers and employees to free us for higher-level tasks; and *embodying* human skills to extend our physical capabilities.

✓ Companies should reimagine their business processes, focusing on using AI to achieve more operational flexibility or speed, greater scale, better decision making, or increased personalization of products and services. Determine which characteristic is central to the desired transformation, how to harness intelligent collaboration to address it, and what alignments and trade-offs with other process characteristics will be necessary.

Adapted from an article in Harvard Business Review, *July–August 2018 (product #R1804J).*

Section 4

THE FUTURE OF AI

10

THREE WAYS AI IS GETTING MORE EMOTIONAL

by Sophie Kleber

I n January 2018, Annette Zimmermann, vice president of research at Gartner, proclaimed: "By 2022, your personal device will know more about your emotional state than your own family." Just two months later, a landmark study from the University of Ohio claimed that its algorithm was now better at detecting emotions than people are.[1]

AI systems and devices will soon recognize, interpret, process, and simulate human emotions. A combination of facial analysis, voice pattern analysis, and deep learning can already decode human emotions for market research and political polling purposes. With companies like Affectiva, Beyond Verbal, and Sensay providing plug-and-play sentiment analysis software, the affective computing market is estimated to grow to $41 billion by 2022, as firms like Amazon, Google, Facebook, and Apple race to decode their users' emotions.

Emotional inputs will create a shift from data-driven IQ-heavy interactions to deep EQ-guided experiences, giving brands the opportunity to connect to customers on a much deeper, more personal level. But reading people's emotions is a delicate business. Emotions are highly personal, and users will have concerns about privacy invasion and manipulation. Before companies dive in, leaders should consider questions like:

1. What are you offering? Does your value proposition naturally lend itself to the involvement of emotions? And can you credibly justify the inclusion of emotional clues for the betterment of the user experience?

2. What are your customers' emotional intentions when interacting with your brand? What is the nature of the interaction?

3. Has the user given you explicit permission to analyze their emotions? Does the user stay in control

of their data, and can they revoke their permission at any given time?

4. Is your system smart enough to accurately read and react to a user's emotions?

5. What is the danger in any given situation if the system should fail—danger for the user, and/or danger for the brand?

Keeping those concerns in mind, business leaders should be aware of current applications for emotional AI. These fall roughly into three categories.

Systems that use emotional analysis to adjust their response

In this application, the AI service acknowledges emotions and factors them into its decision-making process. However, the service's output is completely emotion-free.

Conversational interactive voice responses (IVRs) and chatbots promise to route customers to the right service flow faster and more accurately when factoring in emotions. For example, when the system detects a user to be angry, it routs the user to a different escalation flow or to a human.

AutoEmotive, Affectiva's Automotive AI, and Ford are racing to get emotional car software market-ready to detect human emotions such as anger or lack of attention, and then take over control or stop the vehicle, preventing accidents or acts of road rage.

The security sector also dabbles in emotional AI to detect stressed or angry people. The British government, for instance, monitors its citizens' sentiments on certain topics over social media.

In this category, emotions play a part in the machine's decision-making process. However, the machine still reacts like a machine—essentially, as a giant switchboard routing people in the right direction.

Systems that provide a targeted emotional analysis for learning purposes

In 2009, Philips teamed up with a Dutch bank to develop the idea of a "rationalizer" bracelet to stop traders from making irrational decisions by monitoring their stress levels, which it measures by monitoring the wearer's pulse. Making traders aware of their heightened emotional states made them pause and think before making impulse decisions.

Brain Power's smart glasses help people with autism better understand emotions and social cues. The wearer of this Google Glass–type device sees and hears special feedback geared to the situation—for example, coaching on facial expressions of emotions, when to look at people, and even feedback on the user's own emotional state.

These targeted emotional analysis systems acknowledge and interpret emotions. The insights are communicated to the user for learning purposes. On a personal level, these targeted applications will act like a Fitbit for the heart and mind, aiding in mindfulness, self-awareness, and ultimately self-improvement, while maintaining a machine-person relationship that keeps the user in charge.

Targeted emotional learning systems are also being tested for group settings, such as by analyzing the emotions of students for teachers, or workers for managers. Scaling to group settings can have an Orwellian feeling: Concerns about privacy, creativity, and individuality have these experiments playing on the edge of ethical acceptance. More importantly, adequate psychological training for the people in power is required to interpret the emotional results and to make adequate adjustments.

Systems that mimic and ultimately replace human-to-human interactions

When smart speakers entered the American living room in 2014, we started to get used to hearing computers refer to themselves as "I." Call it a human error or an evolutionary shortcut, but when machines talk, people assume relationships.

There are now products and services that use conversational user interfaces and the concept of "computers as social actors" to try to alleviate mental-health concerns. These applications aim to coach users through crises using techniques from behavioral therapy. Ellie helps treat soldiers with PTSD. Karim helps Syrian refugees overcome trauma. Digital assistants are even tasked with helping alleviate loneliness among the elderly.

Casual applications like Microsoft's XiaoIce, Google Assistant, or Amazon's Alexa use social and emotional cues for a less altruistic purpose—their aim is to secure users' loyalty by acting like new AI BFFs. Futurist Richard van Hooijdonk quips: "If a marketer can get you to cry, he can get you to buy."

The discussion around addictive technology is starting to examine the intentions behind voice assistants. What does it mean for users if personal assistants are hooked up to advertisers? In a leaked Facebook memo, for example, the social media company boasted to advertisers that it could detect, and subsequently target, teens' feelings of "worthlessness" and "insecurity," among other emotions.

Judith Masthoff of the University of Aberdeen says, "I would like people to have their own guardian angel that

could support them emotionally throughout the day."
But in order to get to that ideal, a series of (collectively
agreed upon) experiments will need to guide designers
and brands toward the appropriate level of intimacy, and
a series of failures will determine the rules for maintaining trust, privacy, and emotional boundaries.

The biggest hurdle to finding the right balance might
not be achieving more effective forms of emotional AI
but finding emotionally intelligent humans to build
them.

TAKEAWAYS

AI will soon recognize, interpret, process, and simulate human emotions. Users whose emotions are
analyzed will have concerns about privacy invasion and
manipulation.

✓ Before companies dive into emotional AI, leaders
should consider questions ranging from whether
the value proposition lends itself to involving emotions, to whether customers have given permission
to analyze their emotions, to what the dangers are
if the system fails.

✓ Keeping those concerns in mind, leaders should be aware of the three categories of current applications for emotional AI:

- Systems that use emotional analysis to adjust their response

- Systems that provide a targeted emotional analysis for learning purposes

- Systems that mimic and ultimately replace human-to-human interactions

✓ Companies that navigate these challenges effectively will shift from data-driven IQ-heavy interactions to deep EQ-guided experiences, giving brands the opportunity to connect to customers on deeper, more personal levels.

NOTE

1. Carolos F. Benitez-Quiroz, Ramprakash Srinivasan, and Aleix M. Martinez, "Facial Color Is an Efficient Mechanism to Visually Transmit Emotion," *PNAS* 115, no. 14 (April 3, 2018): 3581–3586, https://www.pnas.org/content/115/14/3581.

Adapted from content posted on hbr.org, July 31, 2018 (product #H04GCW).

11

HOW AI WILL CHANGE STRATEGY

A Thought Experiment

by Ajay Agrawal, Joshua Gans, and Avi Goldfarb

How will AI change strategy? That's the single most common question the three of us are asked by corporate executives, and it's not trivial to answer. AI is fundamentally a prediction technology. As advances in AI make prediction cheaper, economic theory dictates that we'll use prediction more frequently and widely, and the value of complements to prediction—like human judgment—will rise. But what does all this mean for strategy?

Here's a thought experiment we've been using to answer that question. Most people are familiar with shopping at Amazon. As with most online retailers, you visit its website, shop for items, place them in your basket, pay for them, and then Amazon ships them to you. Right now, Amazon's business model is shopping-then-shipping.

Most shoppers have noticed Amazon's recommendation engine while they shop—it offers suggestions of items that its AI predicts you will want to buy. At present, Amazon's AI does a reasonable job, considering the millions of items on offer. However, it is far from perfect. In our case, the AI accurately predicts what we want to buy about 5% of the time. In other words, we actually purchase about 1 out of every 20 items it recommends. Not bad!

Now for the thought experiment. Imagine the Amazon AI collects more information about us: In addition to our searching and purchasing behavior on its website, it also collects other data it finds online, including social media, as well as offline, such as our shopping behavior at Whole Foods. It knows not only what we buy, but also what time we go to the store, which location we shop at, how we pay, and more.

The ideas here are adapted from our book Prediction Machines: The Simple Economics of Artificial Intelligence *(Harvard Business Review Press, 2018).*

Now, imagine the AI uses that data to improve its predictions. We think of this sort of improvement as akin to turning up the volume knob on a speaker dial. But rather than volume, you're turning up the AI's prediction accuracy. What happens to Amazon's strategy as its data scientists, engineers, and machine learning experts work tirelessly to dial up the accuracy on the prediction machine?

At some point, as they turn the knob, the AI's prediction accuracy crosses a threshold, such that it becomes in Amazon's interest to change its business model. The prediction becomes sufficiently accurate that it becomes more profitable for Amazon to ship you the goods that it predicts you will want rather than wait for you to order them. Every week, Amazon ships you boxes of items it predicts you will want, and then you shop in the comfort and convenience of your own home by choosing the items you wish to keep from the boxes it delivered.

This approach offers two benefits to Amazon. First, the convenience of predictive shipping makes it much less likely that you purchase the items from a competing retailer, as the products are conveniently delivered to your home before you buy them elsewhere. Second, predictive shipping nudges you to buy items that you were considering purchasing but might not have gotten around to. In both cases, Amazon gains a higher share-of-wallet.

Turning the prediction dial up far enough changes Amazon's business model from shopping-then-shipping to shipping-then-shopping.

Of course, shoppers would not want to deal with the hassle of returning all the items they don't want. So, Amazon would invest in infrastructure for the product returns—perhaps a fleet of delivery-style trucks that do pickups once a week, conveniently collecting items that customers don't want.

If this is a better business model, then why hasn't Amazon done it already? Well, it may be working on it. But if it implemented the model today, the cost of collecting and handling returned items would outweigh the increase in revenue from a greater share-of-wallet. For example, today we would return 95% of the items it ships to us. That is annoying for us and costly for Amazon. The prediction isn't good enough for Amazon to adopt the new model.

That said, one can imagine a scenario where Amazon adopts the new strategy even *before* the prediction accuracy is good enough to make it profitable because the company *anticipates* that at some point it will be profitable. By launching sooner, Amazon's AI will get more data sooner, and improve faster. Amazon realizes that the sooner it gets started, the harder it will be for competitors to catch up. Better predictions will attract more shoppers, more shoppers will generate more data to train the AI, more data will lead to better predictions, and so on, creating a virtuous circle. In other words, there are increasing returns to AI, and thus the timing of adopting this kind of strategy matters. Adopting too early could be costly but adopting too late could be fatal.

The key insight here is that turning the dial on the prediction machine has a significant impact on strategy. In this example, it shifts Amazon's business model from shopping-then-shipping to shipping-then-shopping, generates the incentive to vertically integrate into operating a product-returns service (including a fleet of trucks), and accelerates the timing of investment due to first-mover advantage from increasing returns. All this is due to the single act of turning the dial on the prediction machine.

Most readers will be familiar with the outcome of companies like Blockbuster and Borders that underestimated how quickly the online consumer behavior dial would turn in the context of online shopping and the digital distribution of goods and services. Perhaps they were lulled into complacency by the initially slow adoption rate of this technology in the early days of the commercial internet (1995–1998).

Today, in the case of AI, some companies are making early bets anticipating that the dial on the prediction machine will start turning faster once it gains momentum. Most people are familiar with Google's 2014 acquisition of DeepMind—over $500 million for a company that had generated negligible revenue, but had developed an AI that learned to play certain Atari games at a superhuman performance level. Perhaps fewer readers are aware that more traditional companies are also making bets on the pace at which the dial will turn. In 2016, GM paid over $1 billion to acquire AI startup Cruise Automation, and in 2017, Ford invested $1 billion in AI startup Argo AI, and John Deere paid over $300 million to acquire AI startup Blue River Technology—all three startups had generated negligible revenue relative to the price at the time of purchase. GM, Ford, and John Deere are each betting on an exponential speedup of AI performance and, at those prices, anticipating a significant impact on their business strategies.

Strategists face two challenges in light of all of this. First, they must invest in developing a better understanding of how fast and how far the dial on their prediction machines will turn for their sector and applications. Second, they must invest in developing a thesis about the strategy options created by the shifting economics of their business that result from turning the dial, similar to the thought experiment we considered for Amazon.

So, what is the overarching theme for initiating an AI strategy? Close your eyes, imagine putting your fingers on the dial of your prediction machine, and, in the immortal words of Spinal Tap, turn it to eleven.

TAKEAWAYS

AI will make prediction cheaper, faster, and more accurate. When the accuracy of predictions passes a certain threshold, it will have a profound impact on strategy.

✓ Strategists must first invest in determining how fast and how much better predictions will become for their sectors and applications. Then they must try to imagine what new strategic options these predictions will create.

✓ Better predictions will enable novel business models that will reshape the strategic playing field in many industries. Industrywide business model reinvention would bring with it strategic concerns such as seizing first-mover advantage and investing in different kinds of capabilities.

✓ For example, an online retailer like Amazon could implement a prediction-based "ship-then-shop" model in which it delivers products to customers before they have selected them. Amazon might begin executing this model before it is profitable to be the first mover, and it might invest further in shipping and logistics infrastructure in order to accommodate the increase in customer returns such a model would generate.

Adapted from content posted on hbr.org, October 3, 2017 (product #H03XDI).

12

THE FUTURE OF AI WILL BE ABOUT LESS DATA, NOT MORE

by H. James Wilson, Paul Daugherty, and Chase Davenport

C ompanies considering how to invest in AI capabilities should first understand that over the coming five years applications and machines will become less artificial and more intelligent. They will rely less on bottom-up big data and more on top-down reasoning that more closely resembles the way humans approach problems and tasks. This general reasoning ability will enable AI to be more broadly applied than ever, creating opportunities for early adopters even in businesses and activities to which it previously seemed unsuited.

In the recent past, AI advanced through deep learning and machine learning, building up systems from the bottom by training them on mountains of data. For instance, driverless vehicles are trained on as many traffic situations as possible. But these data-hungry neural networks, as they are called, have serious limitations. They especially have trouble handling "edge" cases—situations where little data exists. A driverless car that can handle crosswalks, pedestrians, and traffic has trouble processing anomalies like children dressed in unusual Halloween costumes, weaving across the street after dusk.

Many systems are also easily stumped. The iPhone X's facial recognition system doesn't recognize "morning faces"—a user's puffy, haggard look on first awakening. Neural networks have beaten chess champions and triumphed at the ancient Japanese game of Go but turn an image upside down or slightly alter it and the network may misidentify it. Or it may provide "high confidence" identifications of unrecognizable objects.

Data-hungry systems also face business and ethical constraints. Not every company has the volume of data necessary to build unique capabilities using neural networks. Using huge amounts of citizens' data also raises privacy issues likely to lead to more government action like the European Union's General Data Protection Regulation (GDPR), which imposes stringent requirements on the use of individuals' personal data. Further, these systems are black boxes—it's not clear how they use input data to arrive at outputs like actions or decisions. This leaves them open to manipulation by bad actors (like the Russians in the 2016 U.S. presidential election), and when something goes embarrassingly wrong, organizations are hard put to explain why.

In the future, however, we will have top-down systems that don't require as much data and are faster, more flexible, and, like humans, more innately intelligent. A number of companies and organizations are already putting these more natural systems to work. To craft a vision of where AI is heading in the next several years, and then plan investments and tests accordingly, companies should look for developments in four areas.

More-Efficient Robot Reasoning

When robots have a conceptual understanding of the world, as humans do, it is easier to teach them things, using far less data. Vicarious, a Union City, California, startup whose investors include Mark Zuckerberg, Jeff Bezos, and Marc Benioff, is working to develop artificial general intelligence for robots, enabling them to generalize from few examples.

Consider those jumbles of letters and numerals that websites use to determine whether you're a human or a robot. Called *CAPTCHAs* (Completely Automated Public Turing tests to tell Computers and Humans Apart), they are easy for humans to solve and hard for computers. Drawing on computational neuroscience, researchers at Vicarious have developed a model that can break through CAPTCHAs at a far higher rate than deep neural networks and with 300-fold more data efficiency. To parse CAPTCHAs with almost 67% accuracy, the Vicarious model required only five training examples per character, while a state-of-the-art deep neural network required a 50,000-fold larger training set of actual CAPTCHA strings. Such models, with their ability to train faster and generalize more broadly than AI approaches commonly used today, are putting us on a path toward robots that have a human-like conceptual understanding of the world.

Ready Expertise

Modeling what a human expert would do in the face of high uncertainty and little data, top-down artificial intelligence can beat data-hungry approaches for designing and controlling many varieties of factory equipment. Siemens is using top-down AI to control the highly complex combustion process in gas turbines, where air and gas flow into a chamber, ignite, and burn at temperatures as high as 1,600 degrees Celsius. The volume of emissions created and ultimately how long the turbine will continue to operate depend on the interplay of numerous factors, from the quality of the gas to air flow and internal and external temperature.

Using bottom-up machine learning methods, the gas turbine would have to run for a century before producing enough data to begin training. Instead, Siemens researchers Volar Sterzing and Steffen Udluft used methods that required little data in the learning phase for the machines. The monitoring system that resulted makes fine adjustments that optimize how the turbines run in terms of emissions and wear, continuously seeking the best solution in real time, much like an expert knowledgeably twirling multiple knobs in concert.

Common Sense

A variety of organizations are working to teach machines to navigate the world using common sense—to understand everyday objects and actions, communicate naturally, handle unforeseen situations, and learn from experiences. But what comes naturally to humans, without explicit training or data, is fiendishly difficult for machines. Says Oren Etzioni, the CEO of the Allen Institute for Artificial Intelligence (AI2), "No AI system currently deployed can reliably answer a broad range of simple questions, such as, 'If I put my socks in a drawer, will they still be in there tomorrow?' or 'How can you tell if a milk carton is full?'"

To help define what it means for machines to have common sense, AI2 is developing a portfolio of tasks against which progress can be measured. DARPA is investing $2 billion in AI research. In its Machine Common Sense (MCS) program, researchers will create models that mimic core domains of human cognition, including "the domains of *objects* (intuitive physics), *places* (spatial navigation), and *agents* (intentional actors)." Researchers at Microsoft and McGill University have jointly developed a system that has shown great promise for untangling ambiguities in natural language, a problem that requires diverse forms of inference and knowledge.

Making Better Bets

Humans routinely, and often effortlessly, sort through probabilities and act on the likeliest, even with relatively little prior experience. Machines are now being taught to mimic such reasoning through the application of Gaussian processes—probabilistic models that can deal with extensive uncertainty, act on sparse data, and learn from experience. Alphabet, Google's parent company, launched Project Loon, designed to provide internet service to underserved regions of the world through a system of giant balloons hovering in the stratosphere. Their navigational systems employ Gaussian processes to predict where in the stratified and highly variable winds aloft the balloons need to go. The balloons then move into a layer of wind blowing in the right direction, arranging themselves to form one large communication network. The balloons can not only make reasonably accurate predictions by analyzing past flight data but also analyze data during a flight and adjust their predictions accordingly.

Such Gaussian processes hold great promise. They don't require massive amounts of data to recognize patterns; the computations required for inference and learning are relativity easy, and if something goes wrong, its cause can be traced, unlike the black boxes of neural networks.

Though all of these advances are relatively recent, they hark back to the very beginnings of AI in the 1950s, when a number of researchers began to pursue top-down models for mimicking human intelligence. But when progress proved elusive and the rich potential for bottom-up machine learning methods became apparent, the top-down approach was largely abandoned. Today, however, through powerful new research and computational techniques, top-down AI has been reborn. As its great promise begins to be fulfilled, smart companies will put their money where the mind is.

TAKEAWAYS

As AI develops, it will rely less on bottom-up big data and more on top-down reasoning that resembles the way humans approach problems and tasks. This will enable us to apply AI more broadly than ever, creating opportunities for early adopters even in businesses and activities to which AI previously seemed unsuited.

✓ Until recently, most AI advanced through deep learning and machine learning, building up systems by training them on mountains of data. But these data-hungry networks have serious limitations and difficulty handling situations where little data exists.

✓ To craft a vision of where AI is heading in the next several years, and plan investments and tests accordingly, companies should look for the following developments:

- **More-efficient robot reasoning.** When machines have a conceptual understanding of the world, as humans do, it is easier to teach them using far less data.

- **Ready expertise.** Modeling what a human expert would do in the face of high uncertainty and little data, top-down AI can beat data-hungry approaches for designing and controlling many varieties of equipment.

- **Common sense.** Top-down AI will allow machines to navigate the world by understanding everyday objects and actions, handling unforeseen situations, and learning from experiences.

- **Making better bets.** Humans routinely sort through probabilities and act on the likeliest, even with relatively little prior experience. Machines are now learning to mimic such reasoning.

Adapted from content posted on hbr.org, January 14, 2019 (product #H04QN6).

About the Contributors

AJAY AGRAWAL is the Peter Munk Professor of Entrepreneurship at the University of Toronto's Rotman School of Management and research associate at the National Bureau of Economic Research in Cambridge, Massachusetts. He is founder of the Creative Destruction Lab, cofounder of The Next AI, and cofounder of Kindred. He is the coauthor of *Prediction Machines: The Simple Economics of Artificial Intelligence* (Harvard Business Review Press, 2018).

SCOTT BERINATO is a senior editor at *Harvard Business Review* and the author of *Good Charts: The HBR Guide to Making Smarter, More Persuasive Data Visualizations* (Harvard Business Review Press, 2016) and *Good Charts Workbook: Tips, Tools, and Exercises for Making Better Data Visualizations* (Harvard Business Review Press, 2019).

ERIK BRYNJOLFSSON is the director of MIT's Initiative on the Digital Economy, the Schussel Family Professor of Management Science at the MIT Sloan School of Management, and a research associate at NBER. He is the author of several books, including, with Andrew McAfee, *Machine, Platform, Crowd: Harnessing Our Digital Future* (2017) and the *New York Times* bestseller *The Second Machine Age: Work, Progress, and Prosperity in a Time of Brilliant Technologies* (2014). Follow him on Twitter @erikbryn.

JOAQUIN CANDELA is director of Applied Machine Learning at Facebook.

PAUL DAUGHERTY is Accenture's chief technology and innovation officer. He is a coauthor, with H. James Wilson, of *Human + Machine: Reimagining Work in the Age of AI* (Harvard Business Review Press, 2018).

CHASE DAVENPORT is a San Francisco–based technology researcher.

THOMAS H. DAVENPORT is the President's Distinguished Professor in Management and Information Technology at Babson College, a research fellow at the MIT Initiative on the Digital Economy, and a senior adviser at Deloitte Analytics. He is the author of over a dozen management books, most recently *Only Humans Need Apply: Winners and Losers in the Age of Smart Machines* (2016) and *The AI Advantage* (2018).

JOSHUA GANS is the Jeffrey S. Skoll Chair of Technical Innovation and Entrepreneurship at the University of Toronto's Rotman School of Management and serves as chief economist in the Creative Destruction Lab. He is the coauthor of *Prediction Machines: The Simple Economics of Artificial Intelligence* (Harvard Business Review Press, 2018) and the author of *The Disruption Dilemma* (2016).

AVI GOLDFARB is the Ellison Professor of Marketing at the Rotman School of Management, University of Toronto. He is also a research associate at the National Bureau of Economic Research, chief data scientist at the Creative Destruction Lab, and senior editor at *Marketing Science*. He is a coauthor of *Prediction Machines: The Simple Economics of Artificial Intelligence* (Harvard Business Review Press, 2018).

SOPHIE KLEBER is the executive creative director at Huge, where she creates future-forward user experiences to help transform businesses and shape the way we use technology. She is a thought leader in the future of design, has written on behalf of TED, and speaks regularly at SXSW.

MARK KNICKREHM is group chief executive for Accenture Strategy.

VIKRAM MAHIDHAR is the leader of artificial intelligence business at Genpact. He was an entrepreneur and built the AI solutions business at Rage Framework (acquired by Genpact).

EMMA MARTINHO-TRUSWELL is the cofounder and chief operating officer of Oxford Insights, which advises organizations on the strategic, cultural, and leadership opportunities from digital transformation and artificial intelligence.

ANDREW MCAFEE, a principal research scientist at MIT, studies how digital technologies are changing business, the economy, and society. With Erik Brynjolfsson, he coauthored *Machine, Platform, Crowd: Harnessing Our Digital Future* (2017) and *The Second Machine Age: Work, Progress, and Prosperity in a Time of Brilliant Technologies* (2014), which was a *New York Times* bestseller and was shortlisted for the *Financial Times*/McKinsey Business Book of the Year Award. Follow him on Twitter @amcafee.

ANDREW NG is the founder and CEO of Landing AI, the former VP and chief scientist of Baidu, cochairman and cofounder of Coursera, the founder and former lead of Google Brain, and an adjunct professor at Stanford University.

H. JAMES WILSON is a managing director of information technology and business research at Accenture Research. Follow him on Twitter @hjameswilson. He is a coauthor, with Paul Daugherty, of *Human + Machine: Reimagining Work in the Age of AI* (Harvard Business Review Press, 2018).

ROMAN V. YAMPOLSKIY is a tenured associate professor in the department of computer engineering and computer science at the Speed School of Engineering, University of Louisville. He is the founding and current director of the university's cybersecurity lab and an author of many books, including *Artificial Superintelligence: A Futuristic Approach* (2015). Follow him on Twitter @romanyam.

Index